T0068011

# SERMONS FOR YOUR SOUL

Camilla (Denise) Moore

**author**HOUSE®

*AuthorHouse™*
*1663 Liberty Drive*
*Bloomington, IN 47403*
*www.authorhouse.com*
*Phone: 833-262-8899*

*Published by AuthorHouse 12/20/2022*

*ISBN: 978-1-6655-7787-8 (sc)*
*ISBN: 978-1-6655-7786-1 (e)*

*Library of Congress Control Number: 2022922811*

*Print information available on the last page.*

*Unless specified otherwise, all scriptural material of the book is taken from the King James Version of the Bible.*

*This book is printed on acid-free paper.*

# CONTENTS

Acknowledgments ............................................................ vii
Introduction .................................................................... ix

1   It's Just a Smoke Screen .............................................. 1
2   Jesus, the Good Shepherd ............................................ 8
3   Be Encouraged: Your Trouble Isn't Permanent ......... 14
4   Running With the Horses ........................................... 19
5   Have Faith in God ..................................................... 24
6   Who Are You? ............................................................ 30
7   God Will Take Care of You ........................................ 34
8   What's All the Hoopla about a Man Named Jesus? ...... 39
9   Depression Is Depressing ........................................... 47
10  Jesus Teaches Forgiveness .......................................... 53
11  Some Trust in Chariots .............................................. 61
12  You Are Special .......................................................... 67
13  Yes, God Hears Your Prayers (Even When You
    Think He Doesn't) ..................................................... 72
14  God Is Large and in Charge ....................................... 78
15  Nothing Is Too Hard for God .................................... 86
16  What Do You Need from God? ................................... 89
17  Ain't He Good? .......................................................... 98

18   My God, My Provider..............................................102
19   Choosing Your Words Wisely .................................107
20   Worrying Is Worrisome .........................................111
21   God of the Impossible............................................117
22   Lord, I Don't Mind a Little Spit............................ 123
23   I'm in Love............................................................ 126
24   Whose Voice Are You Listening To?....................... 129
25   Don't Freak Out ...................................................135
26   Who Loves Ya, Baby?.............................................139
27   Lord, I'll Take the Crumbs ....................................143
28   O Taste and See .....................................................147
29   Why Me? ...............................................................152
30   The Rapture...........................................................155
31   The Second Coming of Christ................................160
32   Thank You, Lord.................................................... 164


Works Cited..................................................................169

# Acknowledgments

Unless specified otherwise, all scripture is taken from the King James Version of the Holy Bible.

# Introduction

Do you need encouragement and spiritual nourishment? Is your faith in need of a tune-up? If so, this is the book for you. God has more than one way to reach people, and this book is one of them. We didn't know the coronavirus was going to hit the world, but God knew it. We didn't think about Mpox (monkeypox) or polio either, but God knew these viruses would rear their ugly heads too. He told me to write this book a few years ago. He knew it would be needed for such a time as this. When I accepted Christ as my Savior I was instructed to journal. Many of the examples in the sermons come from my experiences which I recorded in my journals (I have a few of them). God also sent me to school to teach me His Word and to prepare me to write *Sermons for Your Soul*.

If the coronavirus, other illnesses, or even your work schedule keep you from going to your house of worship, you can still find some time to spend with the Lord and to grow in your faith. Many churches have virtual services. Numerous pastors are also broadcasting their services on tv, radio and through social media outlets. Others like me have been commissioned to write books. This doesn't mean you should abandon your houses of worship. As the body of Christ, the believer is exhorted to assemble together (Heb.10:25).

*Sermons for Your Soul* came out of years of God giving me sermon topics. At first, I didn't know that's what they were. I didn't know about the plans He had for me. I thought the one- liners were interesting witticisms popping into my mind. I recorded them until one day it dawned on me that they sounded like subject matter for sermons. I decided I wasn't writing them down anymore, and I didn't; that is, until God spoke to me and said, "You're being disobedient!" I apologized to Him for refusing to record them and from that day forward whenever I am prompted to write down what He gives me, I gladly do so.

The first sermon, "It's just a smokescreen," was given to me in 2003 by the Lord. The one liner or topic had been given to me much earlier. This message has special meaning to me because I was on my lunch break at work when I heard the Holy Spirit say, "Sit down and write." What amazes me as I look back on this time is not only that the Holy Spirit dictated the sermon to me, but also that it was given to me in the same sermon format I learned at Nyack College in one of Professor Carlos Perez's classes many years later.

When I finished writing what I was given I said to God, "Wow, you gave me the whole sermon." He answered me saying, "Not quite." God hadn't given me the entire sermon, but He had given me a large portion of it. As time when on He continued to drop more tidbits for me to add to the message. The sermon kept evolving and growing. Now there's enough information for a couple of sermons. God also showed me that the person He has called to bring forth His message has a part in the writing of the sermon, the delivery of it, the personal experiences, the studies, and the style of writing.

This book of sermons is the product of the one-liners God gave me throughout the years. I pray that you will be blessed and encouraged as you read them. If you don't know Christ as your Savior, I pray you will hear His voice as you immerse yourselves in the messages of faith encouragement. I also pray that you will accept His gift of salvation. God is a wonderful and exceptional lover of your soul, and He wants a relationship with you.

# 1

# It's Just a Smoke Screen

For our light affliction, which is but for a moment,
worketh for us a far more exceeding and eternal
weight of glory; While we look not at the things
which are seen, but at the things which are not
seen: for the things which are seen are temporal;
but the things which are not seen are eternal.
—2 Corinthians 4:17–18

There are times in our lives when we will go through storms. Some of you are going through a storm now but be encouraged because your storm is just a smoke screen. Someone may be asking, "What is a smoke screen?" Another person may be wondering, "Why is what I'm going through just a smoke screen?" According to Dictionary.com (2022), a smoke screen is "something intended to disguise, conceal, or deceive; camouflage." What name does your smoke screen have? Is it an illness or a foreclosure of your home? Is it trouble in your marriage or the loss of a business or job? Whatever you're going through, I pray that you will recognize your storm for what it is—just a smoke screen.

Why is what you're going through just a smoke screen? It is a smoke screen because Romans 8:28 says: "And we know that all things work together for good to them that love God, to them who are the called according to his purpose." The scripture doesn't say that some things work together for good. Neither does it say in most cases things work together for good. It says: "*all* things work together for good to them that love God."

Here's another scripture that highlights the Lord's activity relating to our troubles or smoke screens. Psalm 34:19 says: "Many are the afflictions of the righteous: but the LORD delivereth him out of them all." This scripture gives me peace. It tells me that God knows when I'm in trouble and that He will come to my rescue and He will deliver me. For believers in Christ, trials and tribulations are always working for good. God's Word says they are and I believe Him. It may not seem like this scripture is true when we're hurting or in the middle of a catastrophe but regardless of the circumstances God doesn't lie; things are working for good.

Satan wants to use our troubles and our pain to knock us down and to destroy us. He doesn't seem to know that whatever trouble he is allowed to bring into our lives is a weapon in God's hands. God can and does use smokescreens to continually prepare us for kingdom work. Our smoke screens strengthen us and teach us perseverance, integrity, and many other qualities for the work of the Lord. The deceiver is being deceived if he thinks he's gaining ground when he attacks God's people. In Genesis 50:20, Joseph told his brothers that what they did to him was meant to harm him, but God used their evil machinations to save people.

God is still at work saving His people even when we can't see or feel it.

The fact that we may not understand smoke screens can work in Satan's favor. He'll use them to make us fearful or despondent and to distract us. When we do so we're wasting our time because whatever is going on is still working together for good. Satan may have brought trouble to harm us, but if it enters our lives, God allowed it; and according to Romans 8:28 the end result of it will work in God's favor and also ours because our Father will be glorified through the outcome of that thing.

In 2 Corinthians 4:11–18, Apostle Paul emphasizes the truth about smoke screens. He doesn't sugarcoat that we may experience many troubles in the flesh, and he doesn't leave us hanging either about God's intentions concerning them. He points out that God has a greater purpose for our smoke screens. I believe if we read and meditate on the above pericope, we'll grasp Paul's ideology about them. These scriptures tell me that God is in charge no matter what we're going through. It also gives me peace that He's got us—He's got you, and He's got me.

If you're experiencing a smoke screen, don't worry about it. Jesus is in control of whatever your problem is. In Luke 8:22–25 Jesus calmed a horrific storm and then asked His disciples, "Where is your faith?" The Lord wants you to know that He's the master of every storm (smoke screen). He took care of the storm that frightened His disciples, and He'll take care of yours too. There are many reasons why God allows smoke screens in our lives. We may not know why when we're going through them but sometimes, we find out later, as Joseph did (Gen. 50:20). Rest assured that no matter what is happening in our lives, God will bring us through the storm.

Let's be real. Some smoke screens do scare us or make us extremely uncomfortable, and more times than not it seems things aren't going to get better, but the devil is a liar. Did God send His Son to die on the cross for mankind because of His great love for us? Yes, He did. This fact tells me that He has more love for me and you than we have for ourselves. This being the case, we should trust Him and hold on to His promise that He will never leave us or forsake us.

One of our problems in dealing with smoke screens is that we think that the battle is ours when we're going through something. The battle is not ours. It's the Lord's. Joshua had to learn this lesson when God told him to attack Jericho (Josh. 5:13–15). As Joshua approached the city, he came upon a man who had his sword drawn. Joshua said to the man, "Art thou for us, or for our adversaries?" The man said, "Nay; but as captain of the host of the Lord am I now come." What I learned through the man's answer is that we don't have a side. The battle is the Lord's, and as God's children, we are on His side, not the other way around.

I've heard repeatedly that God may not come when you want Him, but He's right on time. The truth of the matter is that God is omnipresent. He doesn't have to go somewhere or come to a certain place. Whether God manifests Himself in your time of need or not, He's always present. Psalm 46:1 says: "God is our refuge and strength, a very present help in trouble." If we could just grasp that He's already present with us, we wouldn't be so easily frightened when trouble arises in our lives.

I would like to share with you a couple of stories in the

Bible that were smoke screens. In 2 Kings 6:8–23, Elisha the prophet continually warns the king of Israel that the king of Aram has made plans to ambush him in a certain place. The Israelite king conducts himself according to Elisha's advice and in doing so avoids being attacked by the king of Aram. After a while, the king of Aram realizes his plans for Israel are being thwarted. Believing there's a spy in his camp, he asks his men, "Will ye not shew me which of us is for the king of Israel?" One of his people pipes up and says, "None, my lord, O king: but Elisha, the prophet that is in Israel, telleth the king of Israel the words that thou speakest in thy bedchamber."

Once the king of Aram hears this, he sends his men to find and capture Elisha, who is in a place called Dothan. One morning, Elisha's servant Gehazi comes outside and sees the city surrounded by horses and chariots. He is afraid, but Elisha is not because Elisha knows about the power of the God he serves. He prays to God - I believe for their protection and so that Gehazi can see what he sees. What did Gehazi see after Elisha's prayer? The Aramean army that came for his master was surrounded by a heavenly host and the Arameans became Elisha's captives instead of the other way around (2 Kings 6). That army was nothing against the power of God. Gehazi didn't understand that the king's attempt to capture Elisha was just a smoke screen. God allowed it knowing full well that He was in control.

In another story, an Assyrian king, Sennacherib, sent Rabshakeh, captain of his army, to threaten and to frighten King Hezekiah and the people of Judah into surrendering to him. Hezekiah was afraid when Rabshakeh showed up, and he tried to buy Sennacherib off by giving him silver and gold. This didn't work. Sennacherib took the silver and gold but sent his commander to Hezekiah a second time with greater demands. Hezekiah was still afraid so He sent word to the prophet Isaiah to petition God on their behalf.

God answered Hezekiah and protected the people of Judah from Sennacherib. He sent to their rescue an angel (only one) who slayed 185,000 trained warriors (2 Kings 18, 19). Sennacherib's attempt to invade and capture Judah was never an issue. It was never going to happen. His threat against Judah was another opportunity for God to show His people what a smoke screen looked like. Sennacherib's failure to conquer Judah highlighted who was in charge, and it wasn't him. It was God Almighty.

One last thing about smoke screens: some of us might not have so many storms in our lives if we stop telling our business. Sometimes Satan knows how to target us for trouble because of our conversations. Have you ever told someone your deepest fears, your doubts, your worries? Have you talked incessantly about a problem, more than you talked to God about it? The words you speak may be used against you. Remember "death and life are in the power of the tongue" (Prov. 18:21).

Satan's not omniscient; he doesn't know everything and he can't read your private thoughts. The only one who can do that is God. Some things Satan may know because he's been around so long and has experience causing trouble for humans. He may also glean information from your conversations with others. Not to worry: God knows what Satan is up to and whatever he does will work together for good because God's Word does not return back to Him void (Isa. 55:11). I pray that you'll learn to leave all of your worries behind you. After all they're just smoke screens.

If you don't know "Christ as your Savior all things are not working together for good for you. The scripture says, "And we know that all things work together for good to them that love God, to them who are the called according to *his* purpose." Do you love Him? Are you born again? Jesus says in John 14:15, If ye love me, keep my commandments." Guess what? You can't keep them without His help. Have you thought about receiving His wonderful gift of salvation? Are you ready? If your answer is yes, let's pray.

Heavenly Father, I'm coming to You for salvation. Thank You for sending Your Son to die on the Cross for me. I want to be saved and I want to never have to worry about where I'm going to spend eternity. I want to live in heaven with You when my life on earth is over. Please forgive me for all of my sins. I accept Your salvation. Thank You for caring for me the way You do. In the name of Jesus Christ, I pray. Amen

## 2

# JESUS, THE GOOD SHEPHERD

Verily, verily, I say unto you, He that entereth
not by the door into the sheepfold, but climbeth
up some other way, the same is a thief and a
robber. But he that entereth in by the door is the
shepherd of the sheep. To him the porter openeth;
and the sheep hear his voice: and he calleth his
own sheep by name, and leadeth them out. And
when he putteth forth his own sheep, he goeth
before them, and the sheep follow him: for they
know his voice. And a stranger will they not
follow, but will flee from him: for they know not
the voice of strangers. This parable spake Jesus
unto them: but they understood not what things
they were which he spake unto them.

—John 10:1–6

In 1995 I moved from Brooklyn to Queens. I still spent
a lot of time in Brooklyn though, because my mom lived
there, and I also worked there. The route I would take on
my way to my mom's home and my job always took me past

a shell of a church. From what I could see, the church only had an exterior; there were no windows, only cutout places where the windows should have been. The doors consisted of boarded-up wood, and the building looked like it had been abandoned for many years. I often wondered what the story was concerning this halted church renovation.

One day I gave a friend a ride home, and as we passed the church, I wondered aloud why it was just sitting there unattended for so many years. My friend stated that she had been told that the pastor of the church stole money from the building fund, which prevented the completion of the work to be done. If what my friend told me was correct, then the pastor of that church was a bad shepherd.

In another story from television, *Broken Vows, Bloody Murder*, 2013, a pastor coerced his teenage son into killing his wife, the son's stepmom, so that he (the pastor) could be free to have a relationship with one of the church members. This pastor was arrested and charged with his wife's murder. His son was also convicted of this crime. The pastor didn't care about his wife, his son, or his congregation. He had to have known that his actions would negatively impact all of them. This pastor was an example of a bad shepherd too.

In John chapters 9 and 10, Jesus teaches His disciples about bad shepherds and good ones. The Pharisees were His example of the bad shepherds. He spoke about their actions relating to His healing a blind man—how they showed no love toward the man and how they were upset with Him because He healed the man on the Sabbath. The Pharisees didn't care about the blind man; they only cared about rules and regulations, in particular that "no work should be done on the Sabbath."

According to Jesus, another thing about bad shepherds

is that they will not risk their lives for the sheep (John 10:12–13). If a wolf came to steal sheep while the bad shepherd was watching them, the predator would have its pick of sheep that day. The bad shepherd would not protect the flock. Jesus called the Pharisees thieves *and* robbers, not one or the other but both. What's the difference between the two? I'll explain with illustrations.

In an article from *Forbes* magazine, Bernie Madoff was arrested and charged with defrauding investors out of around $50 billion (Lenzner 2008). The Jews in Jesus's day would have considered Madoff a thief. The reason he would have been thought of as a thief is that he stole from his investors secretly. Most of them didn't know their money had been stolen until it was too late. Madoff wasn't a robber. He was a thief. An example of a robber was the outlaw, Jesse James. Robbers tend to steal from you outright, in your face, as Jesse and his gang did.

According to Jesus Christ, the Pharisees had the qualities of both Madoff and Jesse James. They'd steal in your face and behind your back, too. In this lesson, Jesus was pointing out the illegitimacy of the Pharisees, who did not know that He was the Messiah—the One they were waiting for. The Pharisees also did not know their sheep—the people they were supposed to guide and show the way of holiness to. Unlike the Pharisees, Jesus Christ is a loving, caring shepherd who is familiar with His sheep.

In John 10:27 He said of His sheep, "My sheep hear my voice, and I know them, and they follow me." This scripture reminds me of an article I read from the *People's Testament Commentary* on Studylight.org. about sheep and shepherds. This article attests to the fact that in Eastern countries the sheep are given names by their masters. The sheep not only recognize their names, but they also recognize their master's voice. If the shepherd called a particular sheep from his flock, it would leave the herd and come to him.

One day a Mr. Hartley wanted to test what he had heard about the Eastern sheep and shepherds, to see if it was true. He met a shepherd who agreed to perform an experiment with him concerning his sheep. He had the shepherd call one of the sheep, who I'll call Isabella, since there was no name mentioned for the sheep in the article, and I'm particularly fond of that name. The shepherd called, "Isabella! Isabella!" Isabella heard her name and left the herd to come to her master.

Mr. Hartley wasn't finished with the experiment. Now he wanted to try something else. He had someone (a stranger to the sheep) change clothes with the shepherd. The stranger now smelled like the shepherd, and the shepherd smelled like the stranger. When Isabella's disguised master called her, she came to him because she recognized his voice. Maybe if Isaac had relied on Esau's voice instead of his smell Jacob wouldn't have been able to trick him into giving him his brother's birthright (Gen. 27:27).

Sadly, as long as we live, there are going to be stories about the unrighteous acts of some pastors/shepherds; and although there are many bad shepherds in this world, all is not lost; there are many good ones as well. We've discussed bad shepherds; now let's talk about the good ones. Before David became king of Israel, he was a shepherd boy. Do you know his story? He tended his father's sheep, feeding them and protecting them from danger.

One day his father sent him to the camp of the Israelite

army to check on his brothers. Goliath the giant Philistine was threatening the Israelites, and they were afraid. David, however, was not afraid. He heard what Goliath was saying to the men and he stepped forward to fight him. King Saul, who was present in body but not in courageous spirit, doubted David's prowess in this matter. To convince him of what he could do, David told him how when a bear and a lion came and took a lamb from his father's herd, he went and took it back and killed them (1 Sam. 17:11, 34–36). David didn't think about his life when the animals came to steal from his flock; he thought about the life of those sheep entrusted to his care. David was a good shepherd.

Did you ever watch the movie *Silence of the Lambs*, from 1991?" In this movie, Jodie Foster played Clarice Starling, an FBI agent who was searching for a particular serial killer. In one of the scenes with Hannibal Lecter, a captured serial killer, Clarice told him about something that happened to her during her childhood. She said that when she was ten years old, she went to live with her mother's cousin and husband, because her father had been murdered. They lived on a sheep and horse ranch in Montana. One morning Clarice woke up early because she heard what she thought were the voices of children crying. She followed the crying to the barn where her uncle and his farmhands were slaughtering spring lambs. She ran to open the gate of the pen to shoo them out, trying to rescue them, but they wouldn't leave the pen. They did not listen to her because they didn't know her voice.

Clarice realized she couldn't save them all, but she thought she could save one of them. She grabbed a lamb and ran. She got about a mile away from the ranch before the sheriff caught up to her and brought her back. The rancher was so angry with her for taking the lamb and running away that he sent her to an orphanage to live. Clarice wasn't a shepherd, but the story she told Hannibal Lecter about her trying to rescue the spring lambs and running with one of them displayed good shepherd qualities. Her mother's cousin and husband didn't have good shepherd qualities. After one act of defiance, they sent Clarice, their ten-year-old relative, to an orphanage.

In today's message, you've read about bad shepherds: how they don't know their sheep, how they're thieves and robbers, and how they won't risk their lives for the sheep. You also read about the qualities of good shepherds: how they love and protect their sheep. The qualities of the good shepherds mentioned above make me think of Jesus Christ. Unlike the Pharisees, Jesus is not just a good shepherd, but He is the "Good Shepherd." What makes this title so fitting for Him? He describes some of His attributes in John 10: He knows and loves His sheep. He says in verse 10, "I lay down my life for the sheep." Jesus fulfilled this prophecy by making the ultimate sacrifice of dying on the Cross for mankind. He literally laid down His life for the sheep, and not just some sheep, but for all of them (John 10:16). He is indeed the Good Shepherd. He wants to be Your shepherd, Your Lord and Savior.

If you are a born-again believer, He already is. If you're not born again, He would like to save you. Won't you please let Him into your life? If you ask Him to save you, He will and you will receive eternal life. You will become a born-again believer, a new creature in Christ. You will also become a part of the church—the body of Christ—and one day Christ will come back for you. At this very moment, He's waiting for you. I pray your answer will be yes to Him. Amen.

## 3

# BE ENCOURAGED:
# YOUR TROUBLE ISN'T PERMANENT

And the Lord, he it is that doth go before thee;
he will be with thee, he will not fail thee, neither
forsake thee: fear not, neither be dismayed.
—Deuteronomy 31:8

Today I would like to offer some encouragement to
those of you who are in a dark place and to the person
who may be wavering in his or her faith. Do you feel like
you're the only one who is sick or suffering? Are you having
financial difficulties or relationship troubles, or are you tired
of waiting for an answer to something you've been praying
for? Whatever is going on with you, just know that God has
not forgotten you, and He is right there with you. Psalm
34:18 says: "The LORD is nigh unto them that are of a
broken heart; and saveth such as be of a contrite spirit."

When you're feeling discouraged let me encourage you
to do as David did in 1 Samuel 30:6. The Bible tells us
that in this passage he encouraged himself. He cried at first,
though. He and all the people with him cried, too. David

might have felt despondent for a while, but he didn't stay parked on "Tears Street" for long. He moved on to "God is my Help Boulevard" because he knew all about God's loving kindness and deliverance from adversity. His experiences had shown him that God would come to his rescue. He did it for him before, and David believed He'd do it for him again. In another instance, Psalm 13:1–6, David was sorrowful for a while, but then he switched gears and encouraged himself. How did he do this? He chose to trust and praise the Lord.

Sometimes it is okay to cry. Crying can be therapeutic. David cried, and the shortest verse in the Bible, John 11:35, says: "Jesus wept." According to Luke 19:41 and Hebrews 5:7 Jesus cried two other times. We're no better and no stronger than Jesus or David. Crying doesn't necessarily mean you don't have faith, and it doesn't mean you're weak. It just means you're hurting, or you're overwhelmed. It also means you're human.

Once many years ago I made an appointment with myself to cry. I had been holding so much pain inside, and I decided that this day I was going to let it all out. I chose a Monday because I didn't have to go to work that day and wouldn't be asked questions about my eyes being swollen or red from crying. I woke up that morning, and I buried my face in my pillow to cry, but that was as far as I got. Although my eyes were wet and the tears were almost ready to fall, I couldn't continue with my plan because my pillow started glowing. I told myself, "I can't cry; I have to see what this is."

While my face was buried in my pillow, I saw myself walking down this long road. I couldn't actually see the road because it was shrouded in a golden mist, but I could feel it under my feet. Not only was the road covered in the golden mist, but everything around me was misty; everything that is except God who was sitting on His throne quite a distance away. I could see the outline of His head, but His face was hidden from me. The throne was big and gleaming of pure gold, and God's arms were positioned on the armrests as He watched me.

While approaching Him I heard Him say, "I'm watching your walk intently." I looked up that word *intently* because I wanted to know exactly what God was conveying to me. Dictionary.com. describes *intently* as "a firmly or steadfastly fixed or directed way, as with the eyes, ears, or mind." Wow, Because of what I was seeing and hearing I no longer wanted to cry.

As I walked toward God, I kept looking at heaps that were lining both sides of the road. Some of the heaps were small, and some of them were large; some were black, and others were grayish. I kept glancing at the heaps wondering what they were until God interrupted my curiosity. He said to me "Those heaps are your troubles and the pain you've experienced. You can choose to look at them, or you can choose to look at Me." I told the LORD, "I choose to look at You." When I changed my focus to look at God instead of the heaps on the sides of the road, those mounds almost totally disappeared. You see, when we focus on our problems things seem worse than they are because we haven't given God the prominence concerning them. We should never think about a problem more than we think about God, the problem solver.

No matter who you are, if you live long enough, you're going to experience some form of pain or adversity. At times things may be great. We'll be enjoying God's unexpected blessings—things so wonderful we can't dream of or imagine them (Eph. 3:20). Other times things might not be going so well. I've heard it said that life isn't a bed of roses, but as I think deeper about this subject, life can be compared to a bed of roses in some respects. For instance, there's the beauty of the rose, the diversity of the many different varieties and fragrances of each kind, and alas there are the thorns. Life is like that; sometimes we experience beautiful bouquets of roses, and sometimes we get the thorns.

In John 16:33, Jesus said we would have tribulation in this world, but He also said that He had overcome the world. There's no need for us to stay bogged down with worry or pain. Apostle Paul says in Romans 8:18: "For I reckon that the sufferings of this present time are not worthy to be compared with the glory which shall be revealed in us." We live in a fallen world, which means no matter how well off we may be physically, mentally, or financially, sometimes the tide is going to turn.

Do you know that some people think that because we are Christians we're not supposed to suffer? That's not true. In 1 Peter 4:12, the disciple says: "Beloved, think it not strange concerning the fiery trial which is to try you, as though some strange thing happened unto you." Peter continues his thought about suffering saying, "But rejoice, inasmuch as ye are partakers of Christ's suffering; that, when his glory shall be revealed, ye may be glad also with exceeding joy." Peter warned us that we will suffer on this earth. Praise God, we won't always suffer; there'll be plenty of good times too.

If you have accepted Christ as your Lord and Savior, your future is extremely bright, and your days of pain will be over permanently at God's appointed time. Revelation

21:4 says: "And God shall wipe away all tears from their eyes; and there shall be no more death, neither sorrow, nor crying, neither shall there be any more pain: for the former things are passed away."

I don't know what you're going through today, but be encouraged and know that your place of pain or struggle is not permanent. It's a stepping-stone to more growth and maturity in God, so don't give up, and don't be afraid to trust Him. After all, He's already said that He would be with us, that He would not fail us or forsake us (Deut. 31:8).

God loves you so much that He sacrificed His only Son, Jesus Christ, to die and atone for our sins. Jesus loves you so much that He willingly died in your place. At His Crucifixion, the soldiers didn't have to break His legs like they did the other men on the crosses. These men would raise themselves up to continue breathing, therefore prolonging their lives (just a little). Jesus was different. He was willing to die so that we could live.

Have you accepted Jesus Christ as your personal Savior? Don't wait to clean yourself up. You could never do what only Jesus can do. His death atoned for all of your sins and through His shed blood you are cleansed (if you accept Him as your Savior). Jesus paid the price for our sins on the Cross, so you and I wouldn't have to. If you don't know Him as your Savior it's not too late; you can have a relationship with Him starting today. Ask Him to come into your heart and to forgive you of every wrong thing you've ever done. Tell Him that you're sorry about them and that you want a new life in Him. He's listening and waiting to honor your request. God bless you.

# 4

# RUNNING WITH THE HORSES

How long shall the land mourn, and the herbs
of every field wither, for the wickedness of them
that dwell therein? the beasts are consumed
and the birds; because they said, "He shall
not see our last end." God answers Jeremiah
saying," If thou hast run with the footmen and
they have wearied thee, then how canst thou
contend with horses: and if in the land of peace,
wherein thou trustedst, they wearied thee,
then how wilt thou do in the swelling of Jordan?"
—Jeremiah 12:4–5

Jeremiah is complaining to God about the wickedness of the people of Judah and how it seems they are prospering in their evil deeds. The people are also plotting against him because he is opposing their sinful behaviors through prophecies from the Lord. Even Jeremiah's own family is in on the betrayal against him (Jer. 11:18–19). Do we, like Jeremiah, complain to God about things going on in our lives? Do we complain to Him more than we praise Him?

In the previous chapters, starting at the beginning of the book of Jeremiah, God had already addressed Jeremiah's concerns telling him what He would do about the wickedness of the Israelites. Jeremiah's complaint to God showed his lack of faith and patience in Him. I can see God asking us similar questions: "If the little problems make you tired, how are you going to be strong when the big ones show up?"

Have you ever made your small problems mountains? A gnat became a giant to you because of your worry about that thing? I have. More than once I've made a mountain out of a molehill. When I started school in 2010, I was given an assignment to write a paper and to turn it in to the professor electronically. I finished the paper on time, but I couldn't submit it. For some reason, it just wouldn't go through. I kept trying and finally reached out to my professor, who just said for me to try to get it in. I tried some more to no avail. I was so upset because I knew at that time that my writing left something to be desired. Also, the syllabus made it clear that points would be taken off for late papers, so for me that was a double whammy.

I sat at the computer with tears about to fall from my eyes. The Holy Spirit spoke to me and said, "If you trusted me, you wouldn't be sitting here crying." When I heard that, I got up from the computer, dried my eyes, and went to my job. I think it was the following week when the professor contacted me and said she still didn't have my paper. I hadn't tried anymore after the first time, but I went back to the computer to try again after she reached out to me. I said something like, "Well, Lord, let me try again." This time the paper went through flawlessly, and although the paper was over a week late, I received an A on it. I was upset about nothing. I had made the fact that I couldn't submit my paper to the professor on time a giant when it was merely a gnat.

David did the opposite of what I did. When it came to Goliath, he treated Goliath like he was a gnat, not a giant. In 1 Samuel 17, David prepared to slay Goliath. He told King Saul to not lose heart on account of that Philistine. David said he would go and fight him. He wasn't worried at all about the outcome of the battle. David was so confident of his success in this matter that he warned the giant:

> Then said David to the Philistine, ""Thou comest to me with a sword, and with a spear, and with a shield: but I come to thee in the name of the LORD of hosts, the God of the armies of Israel, who thou hast defied. This day will the LORD deliver thee into mine hand; and I will smite thee, and take thine head from thee; and I will give the carcases of the host of the Philistines this day unto the fowls of the air, and to the wild beasts of the earth; that all the earth may know that there is a God in Israel. And all this assembly shall know that the LORD saveth not with sword and spear: for the battle is the LORD's, and he will give you into our hands."" (1 Sam. 17:45–47)

David wasn't boasting in his strength; he was boasting in the strength of the Lord.

As long as we live, there will be occasional problems

of some sort. What we need to remember during these times is that God is omnipotent (all-powerful), omniscient (all-knowing), and omnipresent (everywhere at the same time). We don't have to be afraid of anything or anyone. Let's reinforce in our minds Philippians 4:6 which says, "Be careful for nothing; but in every thing by prayer and supplication with thanksgiving let your requests be made known unto God." Another version (NIV) says: "Do not be anxious about anything, but in every situation, by prayer and petition, with thanksgiving, present your requests to God." Let's "cast all our anxiety on the Lord as we are prompted" (1 Pet. 5:7), and let's trust God, remembering that He is strong and mighty, and nothing is too hard for Him. Although God may allow some pain or trouble in our lives, His Word is still true that "No weapon that is formed against thee shall prosper" (Isa. 54:17).

David contended with the horsemen when he confronted Goliath and killed him with a slingshot and a stone (1 Sam. 17:49). Goliath wasn't a problem to David. He knew the battle wasn't his; it was the Lord's. We need to grasp that concept in our lives too. No matter how big our problem is, the battle isn't ours, it's God's and the battle is already won. I pray we learn to see all our problems as David saw Goliath (as a gnat). I also pray that we see our problems and our pain as an opportunity to give God the glory in advance, for bringing us through whatever our trouble may be at the present time.

Heavenly Father, thank You so much for loving us the way You do. Thank You for being our refuge and shield in times of trouble. Thank You for being our Lord and Savior. Draw the unsaved to You, Lord, that they may experience

Your salvation and forgiveness of sins. Show them what they are missing by not accepting You as their Savior and what they have to gain by becoming born-again Christians. I pray they sense the Holy Spirit's prompting to say yes to the invitation for salvation and to then receive the best gift ever offered to them. Thank You, Lord. Amen.

# 5

# HAVE FAITH IN GOD

Now faith is confidence in what we hope for and
assurance about what we do not see.
—Hebrews 11:1 (NIV)

Today I would like to encourage you in your faith.
According to Dictionary.com, faith is confidence or trust
in a person or thing. It also means belief in God or the
doctrines or teachings of religion. According to Romans
12:3, everyone has a portion of it, but this doesn't mean
that God is the focus of everyone's faith. There are those
who trust friends and relatives, riches, and material things
more than and instead of trusting God. Whether we know
it or not, our priority should be to have faith in the Lord,
who is faithful above all else and all others. Lamentations
3:22–23 says: "It is of the Lord's mercies that we are not
consumed, because his compassions fail not. They are new
every morning: great is thy faithfulness."

Charles E. Bennett, a former House Representatives
member from Florida, had the idea to print "In God We
Trust" on the back of our currency. Bennett believed this

statement would "serve as a constant reminder that the nation's political and economic fortunes were tied to its spiritual faith." Although Bennett was well-intentioned, this phrase seems to miss its mark. For some people, God is only thought about when trouble or sickness comes to their doorstep, and I don't know how many people even believe that there is a connection between the nation's faith and our political and economic success. What I am sure of is God's faithfulness toward us. We can't boast about anyone else in comparison to God's love, allegiance, and dedication to our welfare.

Faith in God isn't hard for some, but it is extremely difficult for others. How's your faith in God? Do you believe God can do anything but fail, or are you like the man in Mark 9:24 who cried out, "Lord, I believe; help thou mine unbelief"? If you're in the latter category, don't fret about it. Jesus said in Luke 17:6: "If ye had faith as a grain of mustard seed, ye might say unto this sycamine tree, 'Be thou plucked up by the root, and be thou planted in the sea; and it should obey you.'" With God, even a little faith is a lot.

Getting back to the mustard seed, have you ever seen one? It is so tiny that if you held it in your hand, and it fell to the floor, you'd be hard-pressed to find it because of its size. An amazing thing about this seed is that as small as it is, it can grow to be an impressive ten-feet-tall tree. Jesus's statement about the mustard seed's growth is analogous to how much or how large our faith is capable of growing. Your faith may start small, but it will continue to grow as you continue to walk with the Lord, spending time with Him, praying, and studying the Bible.

Every experience we encounter; whether it be good or

bad, is food to help increase our faith. The Bible is full of stories that depict God's constant care for His children. One of my favorites is the story of Gideon in the book of Judges, chapters 6–8. God chose Gideon to free the Israelites from the persecution and oppression of the Midianites. The Midianites had bullied the Israelites for seven years, destroying their crops and killing their animals. The Bible says because of their fear of the Midianites the Israelites lived in caves, strongholds, and prepared places in the mountains for shelter. Let's read Judges 6:11–16:

> And there came an angel of the LORD, and sat under an oak which *was* in Ophrah, that *pertained* unto Joash the Abiezrite: and his son Gideon threshed wheat by the winepress, to hide it from the Midianites. And the angel of the LORD appeared unto him, and said unto him, The LORD is with thee, thou mighty man of valour. And Gideon said unto him, Oh my Lord, if the LORD be with us, why then is all this befallen us? and where be all his miracles which our fathers told us of, saying, Did not the LORD bring us up from Egypt? but now the LORD hath forsaken us, and delivered us into the hands of the Midianites. And the LORD looked upon him, and said, Go in this thy might, and thou shalt save Israel from the hand of the Midianites: have not I sent thee? And he said unto him, Oh my Lord, wherewith

shall I save Israel? behold, my family is
poor in Manasseh, and I am the least in my
father's house. And the LORD said unto
him, Surely I will be with thee, and thou
shalt smite the Midianites as one man.

This is exactly what happened. God used Gideon to
conquer the Midianites, and Judges 8:28 says: "Thus Midian
was subdued before the children of Israel, so that they lifted
up their heads no more. And the country was in quietness
forty years in the days of Gideon." Some of us are a lot like
Gideon; we can't see the treasure God has placed in us.
We can't see that if we just trust and obey Him, we will be
victorious in what He has called us to do. Gideon didn't
believe God would use him to defeat the Midianites (Judg.
11–16). We're no better than Gideon. We don't always
believe God either.

Many of us tend to believe our friends and family more
than we believe God and what is written in His Word. For
instance, have you noticed how relatives or friends will make
a date to hang out or go to a movie with you, and there's
no doubting for one second that they'll show up? We don't
always put that same kind of trust in what God says. For
example, Isaiah 54:17 tells us: "No weapon forged against
you will prevail" (NIV), yet when trouble arises our first
response is to be fearful instead of having faith that God is
our refuge and our strength. If you have a problem you're
struggling with let that fear be the catalyst that pushes you
to lean on God, and to believe that He will take care of you.
Remember what Jesus said about faith—even if it's small, it
can move mountains.

One way to increase your faith is to start journaling. God is always up to something, and you can't possibly remember all that He has done for you, but if you journal, you'll have a more accurate account of many of the times He's helped you through difficult situations and times when He's given you unexpected blessings. Many of the stories I tell are recorded in my journals so that I won't forget them. My faith has increased because of my journaling, and this book was an unexpected benefit to the practice of doing so.

My job today is to encourage you in your faith, to push you to believe that God will come through for you when you pray about your needs and the needs of others. If you remember nothing else remember this: No problem that you could have is bigger than God. He's all-powerful and can fix whatever difficulties you may be experiencing in your life. Sometimes it might take a while for God to answer your prayers. He doesn't always answer as soon as we call on Him, or the answer may not be what we expected, but He's always listening, and He's always concerned about us.

Think about Gideon and his people; their deliverance took seven years. And have you read what God said to Apostle Paul when he petitioned Him three times about a "thorn in his flesh." God told Paul His grace was sufficient (2 Cor. 12:9). He didn't give Paul a "Yes, I'll do what you ask." He may not give you a yes, either, but know that whatever God has chosen to do about your situation will work for your good. God never gets it wrong, and His timing is perfect, even when He doesn't answer prayer quickly. Why does it sometimes take God so long to answer prayers? Only He knows. There are prayers I'm still waiting for an answer to, but I'm okay with that. Have you ever heard, "Delay does not mean denied?" God is God. He's in charge, and I believe that no matter what happens in my life, He has my back. I believe that He has yours too.

Do you know what else I believe? I believe that if I travel to Africa and while on a boat I trip and fall into a river full of snapping crocodiles, I can call on Jesus, and He'll send angels to rescue me. I'm not saying I won't be afraid. More than likely, I may be screaming like I'm in a contest to see who can yell the loudest, but I'll still be calling and looking to Jesus to rescue me. My thoughts are like those of the three Hebrew boys in Daniel 3:18. If God doesn't rescue me, it doesn't mean He can't and like the Hebrew boys my faith in Him will not be deterred. My mom made me laugh when I told her about my faith belief if I fell into a lake while on an African safari. She simply said, "Don't go to Africa."

There's always the possibility that those crocodiles are the vehicle God will use to bring me to Him, but my job is to believe He'll rescue me. Faith isn't only believing God can do something—it's believing He will. Are you ready for a faith journey? It begins with faith in Jesus Christ. If you haven't accepted Him as your Savior, you can. Ask Jesus to forgive you for your sins and to save you. Tell Him you are tired of doing things your way and want to try His way. He won't turn you down. Amen.

# 6

# WHO ARE YOU?

I will praise thee; for I am fearfully and
wonderfully made: marvelous are thy works; and
that my soul knoweth right well.

—Psalm 139:14

Do you know who you are? I mean do you know who
you are in God's eyes—how loved, special, and unique you
are to Him? Some of us know who we are, but unfortunately,
many people do not. For some individuals, the perception of
who they are is based on their feelings of unworthiness or of
shame about something that God has already forgiven them
for. Others believe the lies Satan or their so-called friends
and family members have told them about themselves. We
are loved, we are special, and we are unique because God
has made us that way. He knows everything about us. He
knows stuff about us that we don't know or remember about
ourselves, and He still loves us and thinks we're special.

When I was a kid, we used the phrase "Later for you!"
to dismiss someone when they said something we didn't
like or didn't want to hear. That was a quick defense to the

one who was trying to disrespect us or hurt our feelings. Sometimes we forget that other people's negative opinions about us are not important. It's what God knows about us that counts, and He knows that we are wonderfully made. We're His handiwork. He made us, and He knows who we are. Because God knows us, He also knows that we sin and that we make all kinds of mistakes. Romans 3:23 says: "For all have sinned, and come short of the glory of God." Do you know people who are always throwing your past in your face? Thanks be to God who sent His Son to atone for our sins through His shed blood on the Cross. His opinion about us supersedes all others.

Our mistakes and failures are not the sum of who we are, and dwelling on them is a waste of valuable time—time we could spend doing something positive. Do you know that the millisecond after you've sinned or made that mistake, it becomes your past? Let the past stay in the past. Negative thoughts are tools from Satan's arsenal. He uses them to beat us down. Unfortunately, he uses people too, and some of them are our brothers and sisters in Christ. Don't get stuck in the negativity of the enemy and don't forget to pray for them (Luke 6:27-28). Don't concentrate on them or what they're doing or saying. God will take care of them.

Do you know that to think negatively about yourself is to disagree with what God knows (not thinks, but knows) about you? It took me a long time to see myself through God's eyes. For many years I was ruled by a feeling of low self-esteem and inadequacy. I never realized how special I am to God. We are God's prized possessions. He sent His Son to die on the Cross in our place. How much love did it take for Jesus to go through what He did for us—the beating, being spit on, the crown of thorns, the humiliation, and the Crucifixion? Christ sees your value. He knows your worth. He wants you to know it too. What Christ knows about you is more important than what others, including yourself, think about you. Genesis 1:27 says that we are created in God's image, and Psalm 139:14 says: "I will praise thee; for I am fearfully and wonderfully made:"

You may not know who you are, but Jesus does. He knows who you are, and He loves you immensely. You didn't do anything to make God love you. He loved you before you were even born. He has made you royalty. Through Christ's crucifixion and resurrection, you have become heirs and joint heirs of Christ. First Peter 2:9 says: "But ye are a chosen generation, a royal priesthood, an holy nation, a peculiar people; that ye should shew forth the praises of him who hath called you out of darkness into his marvellous light:" That's who you are (in case you didn't know).

Apostle Paul didn't know who he was until he had an encounter with the Lord on the road to Damascus. Before that time Paul persecuted Christians and put them in jail. After meeting Christ, he became an instrument to proclaim the Lord's name to the Gentiles, their kings, and the people of Israel (Acts 9:15). Saul thought he was a lowly Benjamite until God had Samuel anoint him king of Israel (1 Sam. 9:10). Rahab, once a harlot, didn't know why she was created. She didn't know that she would be of royal lineage, becoming the great-great-grandmother of King David. David didn't know how important he was to God either. As God's plan for his life unfolded, David was chosen to be King Saul's son-in-law. David thought that was too lofty a position for him. He had no idea that he was going to supersede even that position and replace Saul as Israel's king.

I asked at the beginning of this sermon: Do you know who you are? God does. If you are born again, you are His child. You are blessed and highly favored. You are the head and not the tail. You are above and not beneath. You are God's special treasure, and He has great plans for you. If you don't see yourself in the above sentences ask Him to save you.

Don't put it off any longer. Ask Him to come into your heart and be your Lord and Savior. Ask Him to forgive you of all your sins. He'll do just that. Second Corinthians 5:17 says: "Therefore if any man be in Christ, he is a new creature: old things are passed away, behold all things are become new." If you've prayed for salvation, you have become a new creature in Christ. He immediately accepted your request, and you are now born again. Yayyy! Welcome to the family of believers!

# 7

# GOD WILL TAKE CARE OF YOU

Therefore I tell you, do not worry about your life,
what you will eat or drink; or about your body,
what you will wear. Is not life more than food,
and the body more than clothes? Look at the birds
of the air; they do not sow or reap or store away in
barns, and yet your heavenly Father feeds them.
Are you not much more valuable than they?
—Matthew 6:25–26 (NIV)

In this scripture, Jesus is saying we should not worry about anything because our heavenly Father will take care of us. He uses an example of how God feeds the birds though they aren't as important to Him as we are. We're so special to God that He did something for us that He didn't do for any of the rest of His creation. He created us in His image, and He sent His Son to die on the Cross in our place. It's very comforting knowing how much God cares for us. Second Chronicles 16:9 says: "For the eyes of the Lord run to and fro throughout the whole earth, to shew himself strong in the behalf of them whose heart is perfect toward him." Another scripture, Matthew 5:45 says: "for he maketh his sun to rise on the evil and on the good, and sendeth rain on the just and on the unjust." This passage teaches that the Lord's goodness also extends to those who have not accepted His gift of salvation. In other words, He takes care of them too.

When I was in school, one of my professors divided the students into groups of three and instructed us to choose a nation to pray for. While my group was trying to decide who to pray for, I heard the word "Borneo" in my left ear. I told my two classmates what I heard. They weren't aware of such a place, so we asked the professor about it, and he assured us that there was an Asian island by that name. We had to research the island to find out what problems they were experiencing and what their needs were so that we could pray for them effectively. I learned through that experience just how much God cares for and looks out for people all over the world.

There are so many stories in the Bible about God taking care of His people. He took care of Abraham and Sarah when they arrived in Egypt at the home of the Pharaoh. Fear made Abraham ask Sarah to lie to the Egyptians saying she was his sister instead of his wife because she was so beautiful. Abraham requested this favor from Sarah because he thought he would be killed, and Sarah would be taken into Pharaoh's house. Part of his fear came true; Sarah was taken, but God intervened plaguing Pharaoh's house until he returned her to her husband. Abraham had nothing to worry about. God had them covered all along (Gen. 12:10–20).

The Lord also took care of the Israelites who were slaves

in Egypt for 430 years (Exod. 12:40–41). When their time had come to be released God sent Moses to tell Pharaoh to release His people. Pharaoh refused and continued to do so but after numerous plagues sent from God, he finally realized who he was up against and freed the Israelites from slavery. Unfortunately, later Pharaoh had a change of heart and pursued them to bring them back into captivity. God came to the rescue of the Israelites and drowned Pharaoh and his army in the Red Sea.

All through the years God never failed to take care of His people. When Joshua and the Israelites fought to defend their vassals (the Gibeonites) against the five kings of the Amorites, God was there. The Lord threw these armies into confusion and Israel defeated them at Gibeon. The Bible says that as the armies fled before Israel, the Lord cast down on them large hailstones from the sky, and more of the Amorite armies were killed by the hailstones than by the swords of the Israelites. At Joshua's request, the Lord had the sun and moon stay in their places, prolonging the day until Israel's enemies were defeated (chapters 10 and 11). In chapter 12 Joshua and the Israelites conquered thirty-one more kings and their armies to claim the land God had bequeathed to them. In all of this, God wasn't showing off. God was just being God.

The Lord took care of Elijah the Tishbite when Ahab sought to kill him for proclaiming a drought in the land. God had him hide at the Brook Cherith and instructed ravens to bring him bread and meat in the morning and bread and meat in the evening (1 Kings 17:2–6). God protected King Jehoshaphat of Judah too, when he unwittingly joined ranks with King Ahab to fight against Ramoth Gilead (2 Chron.

18:29–31). Jehoshaphat would have surely died that day had it not been for God's intervention.

The Lord sent an angel to wake Peter up and to guide him out of the prison he was being held in by King Herod (Acts 12:4). The Lord also freed Apostle Paul from prison, but this time He used an earthquake to do it, instead of an angel. Not only did the Lord save Paul, but He used him to tell the jailer and his entire household about salvation, which is a most special act of caring.

Peter and Paul went through difficult times during their ministries, but they never gave up on God. They knew that God is sovereign and that His caring for them included allowing situations that weren't always going to be copacetic. The same thing is true for you and me. After all, how can we grow if we never experience trials and adversities? No experience we go through is wasted with God, and Romans 8:28 is still true; it's all working for good and it doesn't matter if we don't understand how.

What care do you need to give to the Lord? Tell Him about it and believe He'll hear you. Believe He'll answer you according to His riches in glory. I can't tell you how God will help you; I'll just tell you that He will. He's a big God; bigger than any situation you may be facing. There is no better person to trust with your problems than God. Whatever your misfortune may be, He will see about you. He wants to take care of you eternally as well, but to do that, you must be born again.

Have you repented of your sins and committed your life to the Lord? He's waiting for you to come to Him. His Word says: "Behold I stand at the door, and knock. If any man hear my voice, and open the door, I will come in to him, and will sup with him, and he with me" (Rev. 3:20). If you're ready to give your life to Him, ask Him to save you and to forgive you for your sins; He will—that's one of the reasons He died on the Cross. His dying reconciles us to God the Father, but only if you accept His salvation. Are you ready? If so, pray this short prayer with me.

Dear Jesus, I want to be saved. I'm sorry for my sins. I believe that You died for me so that I wouldn't have to pay for my sins. I also believe that You rose on the third day and that you are sitting at the right hand of God, interceding for me. Thank You, Lord, for Your salvation. Amen.

# 8

# WHAT'S ALL THE HOOPLA ABOUT A MAN NAMED JESUS?

In the beginning was the Word, and the Word
was with God, and the Word was God. The same
was in the beginning with God. All things were
made by him; and without him was not any thing
made that was made.

—John 1:1–3

This scripture alone is reason enough for hoopla over
Jesus Christ. He is the Son of God. He's also God and He
is the Creator of the universe (John 1:1-3). He is the second
person of the Trinity, which consists of God the Father,
God the Son, and God the Holy Spirit. He was born of a
virgin. His birth wasn't by artificial insemination or test
tube, either. His birth was a full-fledged miracle and that
too makes Him worthy of hoopla. Jesus was so special that
His future birth was announced to Mary, (His mother) by
the angel Gabriel before she became pregnant. A little later
it was also announced to His earthly father, Joseph.

After Jesus's birth, a star miraculously appeared in the

sky to lead the Magi to Him. Do you know anyone other than Jesus Christ whose location was revealed that way? This star was nothing like the man-made stars on Broadway that the actors and actresses are so thrilled about. This star was a "star among stars." It led the Magi to the very place where the Prince of Peace was, and after it reached its destination, it hung in the sky over Him.

The Magi traveled from the East to see the baby Jesus (Matt. 2:1). They knew He was special though they had never laid eyes on Him before. Nor is there any mention that they previously knew Mary and Joseph, His earthly parents. The Bible says that when the Magi arrived to where Jesus was, they bowed down and worshipped Him. According to Matthew 4:9–10 and Revelation 22:8–9, no one else should be worshipped—only the Lord, God. I am unaware of how much the Magi knew about Jesus when they came to see Him, but they certainly held Him in high esteem. The Bible says the Magi brought Him gold, frankincense, and myrrh. Jesus was worthy of all those gifts, and more.

It took a lot of love for Jesus to leave heaven to come to this sinful world for our benefit. It's so amazing that He left His exquisite home, a place so beautiful we can't even imagine what it's really like. What great love this was and is! There wasn't a lot of hoopla during His birth, but there should have been. In coming to live with us, Christ personified His name—Emmanuel, God with us. He deserves hoopla not only for that reason but because of who He is and all He did and is still doing today.

Jesus is the Lamb of God and the Lion of Judah. He is King of kings, and Lord of lords. Revelation 22:16 says Jesus is the bright and morning star. He is Alpha and Omega, the beginning and the ending. He is our mediator. Romans 8:34 says Jesus is sitting at the right hand of God, interceding on our behalf. It's great to have Jesus as our intercessor, someone who is speaking up for us and reminding God the Father that He took our place on the Cross for what we should be punished for. That's definitely worthy of hoopla. Not only does Jesus intercede for us, but because we are born again, we are now seen in the light of His righteousness. This means that when we approach God the Father, He sees Jesus's righteousness instead of our sinful nature.

Many great men and women lived on earth in times past and even today, but none of them, not even one, closely compares to the greatness of Jesus Christ. While He walked the earth, Jesus performed many miracles. I read in John chapter 2 that Jesus changed water into wine and that it was superior to the original wine designated for the wedding. I don't drink wine, but I think I would have drunk some that day if I had been there. Are you still not convinced Jesus is worthy of hoopla?

He healed the sick of all types of diseases. For instance, He made the blind see, the lame walk, mute people talk, and the deaf hear. Jesus cast out demons, cured a paralytic and a man with a shriveled-up hand. He also healed a bunch of lepers, and cured Disciple Peter's mother of a fever. Jesus cured a lunatic, a man with a mental illness, and He healed a centurion's servant. The servant wasn't even near Jesus when he received his healing. The best thing about Jesus's healing people is that He isn't limited in His healing powers. Human doctors can't heal everything, but Jesus can; if He chooses to do so. He specializes in all diseases and illnesses.

Want to hear some more about Jesus? He told Peter to

take a coin out of a fish's mouth to pay their taxes. The fish hadn't been caught yet, not until Jesus sent Peter to catch it and then retrieve the coin. No one had a chance to slip the coin into the fish's mouth beforehand. Twice Jesus caused fishermen to catch a great haul of fish. The first time was before His resurrection, and the second time was afterward. The number of fish caught was so massive that the nets were breaking, and the two boats full of fish almost sank (Luke 5:1–7).

Jesus walked on the water too. Do you know anyone who can do that? He even invited Peter to join Him. Another time Jesus calmed a raging sea. He once cursed a fig tree, and the next day as He and His disciples passed by the tree it had withered. Jesus put the high priest's ear back on after Peter cut it off during Jesus' arrest. Oh yeah, and what I'm about to say will interest a lot of you, especially if you like to eat. Jesus fed over five thousand people with two fish and five loaves of bread. And can you believe it, there were twelve baskets full of leftovers. Another time, He fed over four thousand people with seven loaves and a few fish. There was food leftover that day too—seven large baskets full. Talk about hoopla.

Jesus came to earth with the assignment to be crucified for poor sinners like you and me, to deliver us from a life of bondage to sin. It boggles my mind that He loves us so much that He was willing to do this, but He knew that without His sacrifice we were doomed to hell. He also knew that without the shedding of His blood, we would never be able to approach the throne of Grace to commune with God the Father or ask Him for anything. Jesus wanted us to have that opportunity.

Adam, the first man, sinned, and his disobedience created a wedge between God and man; a separation that only a perfect sacrifice could mend. Jesus was that perfect sacrifice. The reason Jesus was the perfect sacrifice, and the only one worthy to die in our place, was because He is God, and He is the only person who walked the earth but never sinned. Do you think you could do that? Go without sinning? Could you go without sinning, by your thoughts, your words, or your deeds? Let me answer that question for you. No! No! No! None of us could—but Jesus did.

He died a painful death in our place, and in doing so He paid the penalty for our sins and our sinful nature, which we inherited from Adam. Isaiah 53:4–5 prophesied about Jesus Christ saying: "Surely he hath borne our griefs, and carried our sorrows: yet we did esteem him stricken, smitten of God, and afflicted. But he was wounded for our transgressions, he was bruised for our iniquities: the chastisement of our peace was upon him; and with his stripes we are healed." Jesus bled and died for us, and the blood He shed on the Cross over two thousand years ago is still as potent today as it was back then, and it still atones for all of our sins if we but come to Him and repent of them.

After His death Jesus was buried in a tomb, and three days after that He was resurrected. When He rose from the dead, He walked the earth for a while, and many people saw Him. He went back to heaven, but He didn't leave us alone; He sent us His Holy Spirit to comfort, teach, and guide us in our faith. When I think of all Jesus has done for me, it makes me want to do cartwheels (Oh, how I wish I could). When He went back to heaven, He started preparing a place for all those who have accepted Him as their Savior, and

He's coming back for us (more cartwheels). I don't know about you, but I'm excited about that—He's coming back for me, and He's preparing a home for me.

Some people own their homes. Others rent them, and some people are homeless. For everyone who accepts Christ as their Savior there is the promise of a home waiting in heaven for them (John 14:1–3). We won't have to pay for it or do any renovations on it. It'll be perfect. No home on earth will be comparable to it because no one can outdo Jesus Christ. Furthermore, we are going to live with God the Father, God the Son, and God the Holy Spirit forever. Isn't that fantastic?

In the movie *The Sixth Sense,* 1999, this little boy (Haley Joel Osment) confessed to his therapist, played by Bruce Willis, that he sees dead people. Well, Jesus not only saw dead people, He was one of them, and while He walked the earth, He raised some from the dead. He raised a twelve-year-old girl from her deathbed, and He raised a young man from Nain back to life. Have you heard about Lazarus? He was dead for four days when Jesus called him from death and out of the cave in which he had been placed. When Jesus called him, Lazarus came forth. Do you mean to tell me dead people can hear? If Jesus is the one calling, yes, they can. That's powerful and impressive all by itself. It's worthy of hoopla.

Since the Bible says Jesus healed those people in the Bible, I believe He can heal me. Since it also says He miraculously fed thousands and thousands of people with a little bit of food, I believe He'll continue to feed me. Not only did He do those things when He walked the earth, but He's also doing them today. I'm excited about Jesus, He's so wonderful.

John 20:30–31 says, "And many other signs truly did Jesus in the presence of his disciples, which are not written in this book: but these are written, that ye may believe that Jesus is the Christ, the Son of God, and that believing ye might have life through his name." In the next chapter, verses 21–25, John expounded a little more saying, "And there are also many other things which Jesus did, the which if they should be written every one, I suppose that even the world itself could not contain the books that should be written." I believe this. I've heard many stories about Jesus Christ healing someone or working miracles today.

I'd like to tell you about something else He did that's not written in the Bible. It's a testimony about my mom and, yes, I did get permission from her to tell it. Years ago, in 2005, my mom called me; she was chronically ill with heart disease, and it was a bad day for her. She told me she didn't think she was going to make it, and I was alarmed. She had never said anything like that to me before. I prayed about it, turning it over to the Lord. He woke me up early the next morning and told me to stand proxy for her. He also told me to call out every ailment she had complained about. I did as I was told, and almost immediately after that my body felt drained. I went to bed deciding I was too weak to go to church that morning. I wasn't going to work either, same reason.

Later that night my strength returned, and I felt fine. The next day I called my mom to see how she was doing. She wasn't home, but my brother answered the phone. He said she had gone to the store. I called back a little later. She had returned but went out again. This time I waited until evening. When I called this time, my brother said he couldn't understand it—how she kept going out. He said she had never done this before. I knew, though, how she was able to do this. God had touched her body, revitalizing her. When she was first diagnosed with heart disease, the doctors gave her five years to live. Praise Jesus, more than twenty years have passed since that diagnosis, and she's still here.

Astonishingly, Jesus did so much in such a short period of time, and He hasn't stopped. He's still sustaining His creation today. Bustling excitement and sensational publicity aren't enough to describe the acts of Jesus Christ. I've said a lot about Jesus and the things He did while here, but there's one more thing about Jesus I'd like to mention; He knows men's hearts and He knows what you're thinking (John 2:24). Because of this, some would call Him psychic, but I call Him God.

I mentioned all the diseases and afflictions Jesus healed as He walked the earth, but that's not the total sum of His healing powers. He not only heals physical bodies, but He heals sin-sick souls too. He forgives sin and saves those who come to Him for salvation. He is the only way to the Father; He's the only way we can be saved (John 14:6). If you don't know Jesus Christ as your Savior—someone who loves you more than you love yourself, let me guide you into a relationship with Him.

Pray this prayer.

Thank You God for sending Your Son Jesus Christ to die on the Cross for me. I acknowledge that I am a sinner. I repent of all my sins. and need You as my Lord and Savior. Please forgive me for my sins and come into my heart. Thank You, Lord Jesus, for hearing me and for answering my prayer. Amen.

# 9

# DEPRESSION IS DEPRESSING

Come unto me, all ye that labour and I will give
you rest. Take my yoke upon you and learn of me;
for I am meek and lowly in heart, and ye shall
find rest unto your souls. For my yoke is easy,
and my burden is light.
—Matthew 11:28–30

Today's message is on a topic many of us can relate to.
I'm sure those who have experienced it will agree with me
that depression is awful. For some this painful emotion may
stem from sickness, a broken or troubled relationship, loss
or lack of a job, or bereavement of a loved one. It could also
be the result of a hormonal imbalance or mental illness or
a direct attack from the enemy of our souls, Satan. As you
can see, the causes of depression are numerous. Depression,
though emotional, can feel like physical pain, cutting to the
core of one's very being, and unfortunately no bandage or
salve can make the pain go away.

I believe that everyone experiences some degree of
heartache or pain during their lifetime that could lead

to depression. For some, hopelessness and misery may be fleeting, but for others, their pain is more profound and may last for a long time. If you've never felt this way before, that's wonderful. I'm not on that list. I know about depression. It used to call my name and invite itself to sit with me daily. It had moved into my personal space without contributing to the rent or other household bills.

In my early thirties, I used to pray to die. Nothing in particular had happened for the sadness to overwhelm me the way it did, or so I thought. I realize now after going through it that it was a spirit sent from Satan to keep me bound and to thwart God's plan for my life. Some people wouldn't tell this story, but I must tell mine. I must tell what may help someone else who is in a place of despair and pain. I also tell it because there is hope.

God delivered me from the spirit of depression, and if you're the one I'm talking to, He can heal you too. I suffered two years in silence. My depression was hidden from others because I didn't realize that's what it was. Daily, I was operating on automatic pilot. I didn't appear sad, and I was engaging in conversation, but if later on you asked me what we talked about I couldn't tell you. When I think back during this particular time I felt like I was sitting in a tornado-shaped cone called hopelessness and despair, and I had gotten used to the feeling.

One day in that two-year span of depression I felt good. I went to visit my mom, and while I was sitting in one of her chairs, pain ricocheted all over my body. It felt like targeted lightning. I thought to myself, *God is finally going to answer my prayer.* I hadn't expected to feel any pain when He took me, but I did, and I yelled out, "Lord, I think I changed my mind." The pain ceased immediately, and I never felt that kind of dark depression (or pain) ever again. God had healed me from the depression that dwelt within me for years.

God knows when we're depressed, but He wants us to talk to Him about it anyway. He doesn't want us to be like Asa who relied on man instead of seeking God (2 Chron. 16:1–8, 12). This chapter mentions two times Asa ignored seeking the Lord for His deliverance. God was not pleased with Asa's actions. I'm not saying you can't ask for man's help, but what I am saying is that God comes first; He may guide you to the person or persons He has equipped to help you. Proverbs 3:5–6 says that we should "acknowledge the Lord in all our ways, and he will direct our paths."

If you're suffering from depression, you're not alone. You might be surprised if you knew how many people you encounter daily who are depressed. Many movie stars, musicians, and well-known personalities have suffered or are suffering from depression too. As I listened to the radio one morning while driving from work, the commentator said that because of the pandemic, a larger number of children are having depression issues. Depression does not discriminate, and neither does God. Pray to Him, and wait on Him.

Depression isn't something new. It has been around for ages, just ask Jesus Christ, King David, Jonah, Elijah, and Job. They all felt the tentacles of depression. In Mark 14:34, Jesus is in the Garden of Gethsemane. He is weighed down with pain from the knowledge that His arrest and Crucifixion are about to take place. He tells His disciples, "My soul is exceedingly sorrowful unto death. Luke 22:44 says: "And being in an agony he prayed more earnestly: and his sweat was as it were great drops of blood falling down to the ground." That's a lot of emotional pain. We often think of how much pain Christ suffered on the Cross, but as we see from this verse His pain started before one nail was hammered into His body.

In 2 Samuel 19:1–4, Joab was told that David was weeping over the death of his son Absalom. David covered his face crying loudly for him. His grief was so profound that it affected all the people of his kingdom, and this wasn't his only bout with depression. The book of Psalms mentions David being depressed many times. Have you heard about Jonah, who was swallowed by a whale? He was another person who suffered depression. His depressed state can be seen in his desire to pray for death in Jonah 4:3. Elijah the prophet also prayed for God to take his life (1 Kings 19:3–4). Elijah's depression came from his fear of Jezebel who threatened to kill him as he had killed the prophets of Baal.

A final example of one who was depressed was Job. Job 1:1 says: "Job was perfect and upright, that he feared God and shunned evil." I can understand Job's depression because it appears he did everything he was supposed to do, and yet a calamity of great proportion came upon him unexpectedly, and there was nothing he could do about it. In his distress Job moans, "Why did I not perish at birth, and die as I came from the womb" (Job 3:11–19).

I don't know who I'm talking to today, and I don't know what has caused you to become depressed, but I do know who can heal you of your pain and grief. Jesus can. When we are depressed, we need to turn to Him. He can heal us of anything whether it is physical or emotional. Jesus is the remedy for all our needs, not just the physical ones. Psalm

34:18 says: "The Lord is nigh unto them that are of a broken heart; and saveth such as be of a contrite spirit." I wish I could say He will heal you in a matter of seconds, but I'm not God. He is sovereign, and He decides when it's time for our healing. Nevertheless, He is the one we should turn to before we turn to man for our needs.

The Lord has more than one way of healing us too. Some may be healed through prayer (our praying for ourselves or someone else praying for us). Some may receive healing through the laying on of hands and others may need to see a doctor. Your response to depression may also be the key to coming out of it. Sitting around having a pity party won't work. 1 Samuel 30:6 states that David encouraged himself in the Lord. Maybe he sang hymns, or maybe he prayed earnestly. We don't know exactly how he encouraged himself, but we know his communication with the LORD gave him the courage to go with his men into the enemy's camp and take back what belonged to them.

Depression robs us of peace of mind. One of the things Apostle Paul says for peace of mind is found in Philippians 4:8: "Finally, brethren, whatsoever things are true, whatsoever things are honest, whatsoever things are just, whatsoever is pure, whatsoever things are lovely, whatsoever things are of good report; if there be any virtue, and if there be any praise, think on these things."

In all honesty, it may be hard to think about such things when you're already in the doldrums, but that's where preconceived lists come in handy. If you suffer from depression, constantly go to God about your problem. You should also take advantage of the good days and make a list of blessings from the Lord—times He came through for you in difficult situations. Your list could also contain your favorite scriptures, journal entries, things that made you relax, smile, or laugh. You could also add to this list your favorite jokes or pictures. All these items can be very helpful when the enemy is attacking you. These are merely suggestions, and they are secondary. God should always come first as I pointed out with King Asa.

First Peter 5:7 says: "Casting all your care upon him; for he careth for you." If you're depressed, The Lord can do something about it. He can heal, deliver, and set you free from it. He can also save your soul and grant you eternal life with Him—a life where depression or any other negative thing will not be permitted to enter. If you've never prayed for the salvation of your soul, now is a good time to do so. Pray this prayer with me.

Dear God, I need You. I need Your salvation for my soul. I also need healing from depression. Please heal me and take away the pain. I also pray for others who are suffering from depression. Lord, forgive me of my sins, and help me to live as You would have me live. Thank You, Lord, in advance for total healing. Amen.

## 10

# JESUS TEACHES FORGIVENESS

And if he trespass against thee seven times in a
day, and seven times in a day turn again to thee,
saying, I repent; thou shalt forgive him.

—Luke 17:4

There was once a man named Jerry, who woke up one morning to find himself in a jail cell. Jerry couldn't understand why he was locked up. He didn't recall any actions that would cause him to be put in jail. He also didn't remember blacking out or having some type of seizure that would cause him not to remember what happened to him the night before. All Jerry knew was that this morning when he woke up, he was locked up.

As Jerry sat on a cot in the cell, trying to figure things out, an officer came in to give him breakfast. Jerry pleaded with the officer to release him. He told him, "This is a mistake; I shouldn't be here." The officer replied, with a smirk on his face, "I know, I know, you're innocent. Everyone coming through these doors are." He then walked out to check on the other prisoners in his care. A couple of hours later the officer came back to tell Jerry that he had a visitor. Jerry was confused. How could he have a visitor? Who knew he was in jail? This day was getting weirder by the minute.

As Jerry's visitor walked in to see him, his anger began to boil. "What are *you* doing here?" Jerry yelled at the man. This person was Caesar Jones, his former business partner. Their business went belly up about fifteen years earlier, because Caesar had embezzled thousands of dollars from their company, and the company couldn't recover from the loss. He was arrested for the crime and went to prison. While serving his time, Caesar turned his life around. After being released from prison he became a model citizen. He made restitution for the funds he had stolen and sent a letter of apology to Jerry. Jerry received the letter, but he never responded to it; in fact, he never even read it. He threw it away because he was still angry and resentful about Caesar's embezzlement of funds that caused them to lose their company. Jerry didn't want to hear anything Caesar had to say, so he started screaming for him to leave. Caesar left not having been given a chance to say one word to Jerry.

The next day Jerry's brother Frank came to see him. Immediately Jerry became belligerent, telling his brother to go away, treating him as harshly as he had treated his former business partner the day before. You see, about five years earlier Frank had taken Jerry's brand-new Mercedes Benz without permission and totaled it. The insurance company refused to cover the loss because Frank wasn't listed on the policy, he was driving while intoxicated, and he had no driver's license. That was bad enough but what bothered Jerry the most was that Frank had no job or money to help him get another vehicle, and he never apologized for what he had done.

As Jerry looked at his brother through the cell bars, he wanted so badly to reach through them and strangle him. Jerry hadn't talked to Frank since the day he wrecked his car, and he had no intention of doing so now. He refused to forgive him and he didn't care if he never saw him again. Seeing the anger on Jerry's face told Frank that this was not a good time to talk to his brother. He was truly sorry for what he had done and wanted Jerry to know it. He didn't get the chance to apologize to Jerry during his visit because Jerry went into a fit of rage, yelling for him to leave. Frank left the jailhouse hoping he would get another chance to talk to his brother once he was released and was able to go home.

After lunch, another man came to see Jerry. Jerry recognized him and was ecstatic to see him. It was Jesus Christ. Finally, he thought, "Someone's here that I do want to see!" Jerry knew if anyone could get him out of jail, Jesus could. Jerry pleaded his case with Jesus, telling him how he was unlawfully imprisoned and that no one had told him why he was there. Jesus looked at Jerry and saw the pain and confusion he was feeling. He felt compassion for him and explained to Jerry that the bars that held him in jail were bars of his own making—bars made of unforgiveness.

Jesus further stated that sometimes the effects of unforgiveness is subtle. He showed Jerry how he had held on to resentment for his former business partner and his brother so long that he had created his own jail cell. Jesus helped Jerry to understand that not forgiving Caesar and Frank was like saying that what they did to him is worse than what we do to God every day. It also disrespects Jesus's act of forgiveness of dying on the Cross in our place. Romans 5:8 says God forgave us while we were sinners, yet we have the nerve to not forgive others who sin against us. Who are we to decide who is and isn't worthy of forgiveness, and where would we be if Christ didn't forgive us for our sins? Jesus told Jerry a parable to drive home what he wanted him to understand about unforgiveness:

> ""Therefore is the kingdom of heaven likened unto a certain king, which would take account of his servants. And when he had begun to reckon, one was brought unto him, which owed him ten thousand talents. But forasmuch as he had not to pay, his lord commanded him to be sold, and his wife, and children, and all that he had and payment to be made. The servant therefore fell down, and worshipped him, saying, "Lord, have patience with me, and I will pay thee all." Then the lord of that servant was moved with compassion, and loosed him, and forgave him the debt. But the same servant went out, and found one of his fellowservants, which owed him an hundred pence: and he laid hands on him, and took him by the throat, saying, "Pay me that thou owest." And his fellowservant fell down at his feet, and besought him, saying, "Have patience with me, and I will pay thee all." And he would not: but went and cast him into prison, till he should pay the debt.

So when his fellowservants saw what was done they were very sorry, and came and told unto their lord all that was done. Then his lord, after that he had called him, said unto him, O thou wicked servant, I forgave thee all that debt, because thou desiredst me: shouldest not thou also have had compassion on thy fellowservant, even as I had pity on thee? And his lord was wroth, and delivered him to the tormentors, till he should pay all that was due unto him.""

(Matthew 18:23–34)

Do you know what Jesus says in verse 35 of this chapter? (It's a kicker). He says, "This is how my heavenly Father will treat each of you unless you forgive your brother or sister from your heart" (NIV). This shows that God is displeased if we don't forgive others. In Matthew 18:21–22, Peter asks Jesus how many times he should forgive his brother if he sins against him. Jesus told Peter to forgive his brother seventy times seven—490 times. Jesus isn't giving a solid number for forgiving someone. He's saying forgive the offender every time—*every single time*!

When Jesus concluded the parable, Jerry broke down crying, because he now understood how unforgiveness toward his business partner and his brother had affected his life and his relationship with the Lord. Jerry asked Jesus to forgive him for his disobedience and to help him forgive them, which Jesus did. As soon as Jerry asked Jesus to forgive him for the hardness of his heart toward Frank and Caesar, his heart softened and the doors of his jail cell flung open. Jerry walked out of the building feeling as light as a feather.

Are you holding on to unforgiveness of something someone did to you? If you are, then you're just like Jerry. He couldn't forgive Frank and Caesar just the one time they wronged him. If you're holding on to unforgiveness, you are carrying unnecessary weight, and more importantly, you're being disobedient to Jesus Christ. He teaches that we should always forgive the person who has wronged us. Jesus isn't telling Peter (and us) to do something He doesn't do every day. If we try to compute how many times He has forgiven sins of just one person, it is an astronomical number. He started forgiving people before He died. He forgave the thief on the Cross next to Him, Mary Magdalene, the paralyzed man in Luke 7:48, and numerous individuals not mentioned by name. Jesus Christ even forgave those who mistreated Him and nailed Him to the cross, and He forgives you and I daily.

This story is fictitious, but all over the world, there are people like Jerry who are bound by their chains of unforgiveness of someone they feel has wronged them. Do we want to be like Jerry, or do we want to be like Jesus? Unforgiveness is a wound you control the healing for. Are you refusing to be healed, or are you letting unforgiveness fester and get worse? Nelson Mandela said "Unforgiveness is like drinking poison and then hoping it kills your enemy."

Marlene Dietrich, a leading lady of film in the 1930's and 1940's addressed another part of forgiveness. She said, "Once a woman has forgiven her man, she must not reheat his sins for breakfast." She's saying if you forgive someone don't continue to throw what they did to you back in their face.

I have a pet peeve concerning forgiveness. When you feel the desire to apologize to someone, don't start the apology with, "If I did something or said something to hurt you ..…." If you're apologizing to someone, you already know you did or said something that may have hurt or offended that person. Throw that prideful "if" out of the window. Give a humble apology. This is pleasing to God, and it shows you are truly sorry.

Let's examine ourselves to make sure we're being obedient to Jesus Christ by forgiving others their trespasses. Let's please the Lord by letting go of grudges and offenses against others. None of us are perfect. We're not qualified to withhold forgiveness from anyone. We're not God, and while you're at it, forgive yourself too. So many people beat themselves up over past sins and/or mistakes. Stop holding on to the things you did a long time ago. It's water under the bridge.

Forgiving someone isn't always easy, but know this; God doesn't ask you to do anything He hasn't enabled you to do and He will help you. Jesus wants us to forgive others: relatives, strangers, acquaintances, and ourselves too. Sometimes people don't even realize they have hurt you. Maybe that's the reason for Matthew 18:15, which instructs the person who is hurt to approach the person who hurt them. This verse teaches a different route of forgiveness: You're going to the person who hurt you instead of waiting for that person to come to you.

So now, what are you going to do? It's up to you; as they say, "The ball is in your court." Let's follow the golden rule of Matthew 7:12, which says: "Therefore all things whatsoever ye would that men should do to you, do ye even so to them: for this is the law and the prophets." For the record, if you believe you have forgiven someone, but you still feel uncomfortable when you're around them, don't worry about it. This just means it still bothers you. It may take a while for you not to feel angry, hurt, or sad about what transpired. Trust God in this matter. I believe that at His appointed time He will heal your heart from the pain of what happened to or against you. Have you been forgiven for your sins? Have you asked Jesus Christ to come into your heart and be your Savior? Do you want to? If so, pray this prayer with me.

Dear Lord, I am sorry for my sins. Please forgive me, and come into my life. LORD, as You've forgiven me, help me to forgive others. Thank You, Father, for all You do. In Jesus's name, I pray. Amen.

## 11

# SOME TRUST IN CHARIOTS

Some trust in chariots, and some in horses: but we will remember the name of the LORD our God.
—Psalm 20:7

Psalm 20:7 is a prayer of David in which he declares that he and his people will trust in God rather than in chariots and horses. This phrase may be better understood today that they will depend on God rather than relying on the power of the military force of the nation. In ancient times, some leaders actually did trust in chariots and horses. Isaiah warned the Jews about doing this in chapter 31:1. To put anything before God is to make that thing an idol. In Exodus 20:3 God tells the Israelites they should have no other gods before Him. Nothing should take God's place in our lives. That was a command for the Israelites and it is a command for us too. God is our Source and the things He blesses us with are resources.

Psalm 46:1 says: "God is our refuge and strength, A very present help in trouble." God should always be our first thought in the good times and in the bad. Because

He is our refuge and strength, we should definitely turn to Him when difficulties arise in our lives. Proverbs 3:5 says: "Trust in the LORD with all thine heart; and lean not unto thine own understanding." Do *you* know something about trusting God? King David did. He always depended upon God for his deliverance, no matter what dangerous or painful situations arose in his life.

David trusted God when he fought Goliath. He leaned on Him when King Saul and his son Absalom pursued him to take his life. He trusted God when he fought a lion and a bear. He trusted God for mercy when he made that huge mistake of taking a census of the Israelites in 1 Chronicles 21:2 and 7–13. In case you don't know the story, David sent Joab, his commander in chief, to number the tribes of Israel. He wanted to know how many fighting men he had.

Joab tried to talk David out of his folly; he knew it was evil toward God. Joab also knew that it didn't matter how many men were in their armies. The Israelites won their battles because of God's intervention, not because of the number of troops there were. David refused to listen to Joab in this matter. He was what some would call bullheaded. Later, God sent someone to David that he *would* listen to: Gad the prophet. Through the prophet God gave David three choices of punishment for what he had done. David chose to fall into the hands of the Lord. (1 Chron. 21:7–13). He trusted God for his chastisement.

Moses was another person who trusted the Lord. God told him to go to the Pharaoh of Egypt to demand that he let His people go. Moses did as he was instructed, time and time again. The Israelites were slaves in Egypt, for 400–430 years, and now their time of deliverance had come. What

Moses had to say to Pharaoh went against Pharaoh's plans for the Israelites because he needed their free labor. He was not releasing the children of Israel from bondage. Who would replace them? Too bad he didn't trust God. If he had he would not have drowned in the Red Sea.

Because of his stubbornness of heart, Pharaoh and a lot of his people lost their lives. All the firstborn of Egypt were slain by the angel of death the night of the Passover, but none of the Israelite's firstborn died. Some trust in chariots, but Moses and the Israelites trusted in God.

Joseph's faith never waned either, even though he was sold as a slave in Egypt, falsely accused of attempted rape and remanded to prison for many years. Daniel, a Hebrew boy, trusted God when he was thrown into a lion's den. God told Noah to build an ark. He trusted God and built it. He told Abraham to kill his son. He trusted God and was prepared to do so until stopped by an angel.

I've named a lot of men, but women trusted God too. Moses's mother, Jochebed, is commended in Hebrews 11:23 for trusting God. She defied the king's edict to kill her newborn son, Moses, and hid him as long as she could. Because of her defiance to the king's decree, Moses lived and freed the children of Israel from slavery. Deborah the prophetess and judge of Israel accompanied Barak to war against Sisera and all his chariots and army. They were victorious in this battle. Deborah knew they would be because she trusted God. Esther trusted God too and because of her faith she prevented her people from being annihilated. Another woman, Mary, trusted God when He announced to her through the angel Gabriel that she would give birth to His son, Jesus Christ, although she was a virgin.

Jesus Christ said in Matthew 6:26, "Behold the fowls of the air: for they sow not, neither do they reap, nor gather into barns; yet your heavenly Father feedeth them. Are ye not much better than they?" Jesus is saying here that we should trust the Father for our needs. Jesus Christ trusts God the Father, and we should trust Him too. Do you trust humans or things more than you trust God?

I learned at an early age to trust God. My siblings and I were raised in the church. We had to go to Sunday school and church each week, and I can't remember ever missing a Sunday. We were taught about God the Father, God the Son, and God the Holy Spirit. I was about thirteen or fourteen when I started seriously questioning what I had been taught in Sunday school, and one day I said to God, "I don't know if that stuff is true. God, if you're real, let me find pennies as I walk to the store."

Some people might think that my asking God to let me find pennies and finding them was nothing, even childish, (I *was* a child) but it was important to me, and as I continued to walk, I also continued to ask God to let me find pennies. I kept finding them, and they weren't all clustered together either. I found penny after penny until I acknowledged God was communing with me. I never needed another affirmation that God is real. That simple answer to prayer about the pennies sealed it for me, and I never doubted God's existence again. I still didn't get saved at that time, but praise Jesus, I was on my way because now I knew He was real.

I ran across this poem that I thought very insightful about trusting God. The poem is called "Overheard in an Orchard," written by Elizabeth Cheney in 1859. It reads:

Said the robin to the sparrow,
"I should really like to know,
Why these anxious human beings
Rush about and worry so."
Said the sparrow to the robin,
"Friend I think that it must be,
That they have no Heavenly Father,
Such as cares for you and me."

Matthew 7:7–8 says: "Ask, and it shall be given you; seek, and ye shall find; knock, and it shall be opened unto you: For every one that asketh receiveth; and he that seeketh findeth; and to him that knocketh it shall be opened." Praying to God regularly can develop trust in Him. When we pray, we're looking to Him for help. We may not get all that we pray for, and our prayers may not be answered the way we would like, but our needs will be met. Philippians 4:19 says: "But my God shall supply all your need according to his riches in glory by Christ Jesus." As we continue to mature in our faith, we begin to see that God really can be trusted to take care of us.

If you want a better quality of life; don't trust in chariots and horses. Don't have total confidence in your paycheck or bank account, good health, family or friends. At some point they will let you down. Put your complete trust in God. He's omnipotent, omniscient, and omnipresent. He can do anything; He knows everything, and He's everywhere at the same time. After reading this sermon I'd like to ask you, "Who are you going to trust?" If your answer is God, then this means you are already born again or you are ready to accept Christ's gift of salvation. If that's the case, pray this prayer with me:

Lord, I am a sinner, but I don't want to be. Forgive me for all my sins and save me. I believe that You sent Your son to die on the Cross for me. Thank You, Jesus, for this amazing act of Your love. I want eternal life and the opportunity to live with You forever. Thank You so much for Your salvation. Amen.

# 12

# YOU ARE SPECIAL

O lord, thou hast searched me, and known me.
Thou knowest my downsitting and mine uprising,
thou understandest my thought afar off. Thou
compassest my path and my lying down, and art
acquainted with all my ways. For there is not a
word in my tongue, but, lo, O Lord, thou knowest
it altogether. Thou hast beset me behind and
before, and laid thine hand upon me.
—Psalm 139:1–5

For thou hast possessed my reins: thou hast
covered me in my mother's womb.
I will praise thee; for I am fearfully and
wonderfully made: marvellous are thy works; and
that my soul knoweth right well.
—Psalm 139:13–14

After reading these verses, can you grasp how special
you are to God? Do you need more convincing? Matthew
10:29–31 says: "Are not two sparrows sold for a farthing?

and one of them shall not fall on the ground without your Father. But the very hairs of your head are all numbered. Fear ye not therefore, ye are of more value than many sparrows." You're so special that God knows how many hairs are on your head. Do you have children, relatives, or that special loved one? Do you know how many hairs are on their heads? What about their eyelashes? God knows this for every single one of us. That tells me that we're special.

Sometimes our belief of who we are is not a true representation of who God says we are. Are we seeing ourselves in His eyes or through the eyes of someone else? Sometimes we're our own worst enemy. Dwelling on our past can also be the culprit that hinders our ability to see how special we are to God. It took me a long time to see myself through God's eyes. For many years I was ruled by a feeling of low self-esteem. That was a trick of the enemy to keep me from soaring to greater heights, to be all that God has called and created me to be.

We are the prized possessions of God, and He has given all of us gifts and/or talents. Through the crucifixion of Jesus Christ, we are redeemed from the bondage of sin. He wasn't only nailed to a cross but He suffered before His death. He was whipped, spit on, and a crown of thorns was pressed into His scalp. You are extremely special and loved to have someone suffer and die like that in your place. Jesus Christ did that for mankind. His death atoned for all our sins— past, present, and future ones. The blood He shed for the remission of sins has stretched over the centuries to include you and me, who weren't even born when He died. What amazing grace. What amazing love.

I praise God and I thank Him for considering me

special, for seeing the righteousness of Christ when He looks at me instead of a list of my trespasses. We're all special to God, not just me but you too. Do you know how special you are to Him? If your answer is yes, that's great. But if your answer is no, or if you're not sure about your status with Him, I would like to turn my attention to you.

Do you suffer from low self-esteem? Do you beat yourself up when you make a mistake or make a bad decision? If you do, you're helping Satan hold you back, you're helping him make you feel bad, too. So stop it! Stop helping Satan do his job! He is the accuser. He is the one who criticizes or condemns you. Your accuser or criticizer may look like a person but it's Satan using them. When you fall short of God's glory, and we all do (Rom. 3:23), God doesn't beat you up. He will be there with open arms to welcome you back like the father did to the prodigal son (Luke 15:11-32), so apologize to God for whatever you did and keep it moving. What you did in the past is the past, even if it was only a few minutes ago. You can't change it, so don't dwell on it. That's a waste of time.

When I was new in the Lord and would do something that I shouldn't have, I would feel so bad that I would beat myself up over that thing, thinking about how I sinned. It would stay on my mind sometimes for days. I thought dwelling on my sin would show God that I was sorry about what I had done. I didn't think of how God knows everything—how He knew what I would do before I did it and how He already knew I was sorry for what I had done. I didn't need to spend my day in misery or doing penance (voluntary self-punishment) for my sin. That's not the life

God wants for me or you to live. We don't have to pay a price for our sins; Jesus already did that.

What we can do to honor Jesus Christ is not to dwell on our sins but to believe God's Word and to do our best to obey Him. We are not alone in our walk of faith. The Holy Spirit is always guiding us and teaching us how to live holy. We are special to God. He knows who we are, and He loves us. That's right. He knows us and loves us, and that makes us special.

Nothing we can do can change His love for us either. How do I know this? Romans 8:38–39 says so. I think we need to read this aloud: "For I am persuaded, that neither death, nor life, nor angels, nor principalities, nor powers, nor things present, nor things to come, nor height, nor depth, nor any other creature, shall be able to separate us from the love of God, which is in Christ Jesus our Lord." Another scripture says: "See what great love the Father has lavished on us, that we should be called children of God" (1 John 3:1a NIV). I like the word *lavish* in the description of the way God pours out His love on us. It makes me feel like He has smeared His love all over us.

Sometimes people have a hard time saying, "I love you". God is different. He wants us to know that He loves us. He tells us in His Word that He does. His actions scream that He loves us and because of this I have no doubt that we are special to Him. God gave His Son to take our place for punishment. We're special. We belong to a chosen generation. We're special (2 Pet. 2:9). God saw fit to create us in His image. We're special. The fact that nothing can separate us from His love lets me know that we are exceedingly special to Him.

I asked this question before but I want to ask it again. Can you grasp how special you are to God? God created you and wants a relationship with you. God has singled you out for eternal life. He has given you special talents and gifts. He's fed and clothed you. He's protected you for years and even while you were in your mother's womb you were looked after. The Bible says so much about how special we are. Are you going to believe God's Word? We're all special because God created us, but there's a deeper level to be obtained through God's gift of salvation. He wants to love you throughout eternity. That can only happen if you take the step to become a born-again Christian.

Acknowledge Jesus Christ as God's Son, the one who died on the Cross for you, and accept Him as your Savior. He will forgive you of all your sins, if you ask Him to? Come on, enter the most wonderful relationship you'll ever experience. Romans 10:9 says: "If you declare with your mouth, 'Jesus is Lord,' and believe in your heart that God raised him from the dead, you will be saved." I pray that you've accepted Christ as your Savior. If you haven't, it's not too late. He's waiting for you. What's your answer?

## 13

# YES, GOD HEARS YOUR PRAYERS (EVEN WHEN YOU THINK HE DOESN'T)

For the eyes of the Lord are over the righteous,
and his ears are open unto their prayers: but the
face of the Lord is against them that do evil.
—1 Peter 3:12

When it seems like God isn't listening to your prayers, keep praying anyway, because He is listening. And when you've prayed and prayed and cried and cried about your situation, and you have received no answer, pray some more. Continue to hold on to the expectation that God is going to answer your prayers. Don't let Satan fool you into thinking that God doesn't hear you or that He's not concerned about you. This isn't true. John 3:16 says: "For God so loved the world, that he gave his only begotten Son, that whosoever believeth in him should not perish, but have everlasting life." God sacrificing His only Son to atone for our sins and offering us everlasting life in His presence is a whole lot of love. Because He loves us so much, He is truly attentive to our prayers.

Have you seen the movie *Bruce Almighty*, from 2003, in which Bruce (Jim Carrey) complains to God that he's not being treated fairly? Morgan Freeman, who plays the role of God, offers Bruce all his powers if Bruce thinks he can do a better job than he can. The bottom line is Bruce can't do a better job than God (Freeman); he doesn't even come close, but we already knew that was going to be the case, even without knowing the end of the movie, didn't we?

At one point in the movie, Bruce is hearing prayers from people all over the world, and they're all praying at the same time. He tries to answer all the prayers, but his efforts are futile. The prayers never stop, and Bruce can't keep up with answering them. He isn't even giving each person who's praying his undivided attention.

Aren't you glad God is not like Bruce? He always hears your prayers. He has no limitations on hearing them or answering them, even if billions of people all over the world pray to Him at the same time. God is Almighty, and He can hear and solve any problem you bring to Him. You're important to the LORD, and whatever you need from Him, just ask, and wait on Him. Psalm 27:14 says: "Wait on the LORD: be of good courage, and he shall strengthen thine heart: wait, I say, on the LORD." Another scripture, Isaiah 40:31, says: "But they that wait upon the LORD shall renew their strength; they shall mount up with wings as eagles; they shall run and not be weary; they shall walk and not faint."

In these scriptures, God is not specifically telling you how He's going to strengthen you. Perhaps He'll send encouragement from someone, or someone will pray for you. He could deliver you from that problem just the way you want Him to, or He could solve it in a way you never imagined. We may not like it, but God could also let us languish in a problem until we grasp whatever lesson He wants us to learn. However He chooses to answer your prayer is His business, not yours. However long He takes to answer it is not your business, either. It's His. Your business is to believe that no matter what the situation, the Lord can solve your problem, and He is going to come through for you.

I've prayed to God many times, and sometimes He has answered my prayers quickly, and other times it has taken years for me to receive an answer. When I wanted to go to Israel and Cuba, God answered my prayers quickly, giving me the finances to pay for the trips. When I prayed about my right eye, well, that was another story. I had injured my eye while pulling buckets apart on my job in 1996. I pulled so hard that the bucket loosened and traveled straight to my eye, damaging it and causing excruciating pain.

I prayed to God for healing, and I went to the doctor too, but the medicine that the doctor put in it made the condition worse instead of better. I never went back to her again. I kept praying to God about it though. Many times, and for many years, I would wake up feeling as if broken glass was under the eyelid, scratching my eyeball each time it moved. Slowly, as time went on, my eye got better.

Wouldn't you know it, as I decided to use this story as an example about delayed prayer in this sermon, the eye started giving me trouble again. It hadn't bothered me for a long time. I recognized what was going on, and I quoted a phrase Joyce Meyer spoke years ago on one of her TV broadcasts concerning her husband, Dave. She said that Satan was trying to negate one of Dave's blessings, and Dave said, "Satan I see you, and I am not impressed." What she said stuck with me, and from time to time I tell Satan the same thing. This was one of those times. He was not going to make me believe that I wasn't healed. I didn't give up praying to God about it and thanking Him for healing me. Don't you give up either. God knows what He's doing.

Have you read the book of Job? The Bible says in Job 1:1 that he was perfect and upright, that he feared God and abstained from evil. It appears there was nothing more Job could have done to please God, yet he was assailed by the most horrendous problems you could think of. All ten of his children were killed, he lost his wealth, his body was wracked with painful sores from head to toe, and his friends blamed and criticized him for what was going on in his life instead of uplifting and comforting him.

Admirably, Job didn't give up on God despite all his troubles. Instead, he made up his mind that he was going to continue holding on to Him. His exact words in Job 13:15 were, "Though he slay me, yet will I trust him." Job didn't understand why he was being targeted for what seemed like destruction, but he did understand that God still loved him and he continued to love God. Job never stopped trusting God for his deliverance, and as the story goes, one day he received his healing. Not only did God heal Job, but He restored his wealth twofold and gave him ten more children, the same number that had died during the calamity.

Do you ask for God's help when you're in trouble, but instead of waiting on the Lord for your answer, you're impatient and want the prayers answered quickly? Many years ago, I remember hearing Bishop Neil Ellis say on a television program that we want God to cheat. He said we want Him to give us the answers to the test before we complete it. What a true statement! We don't want to suffer, but it's a part of life. Jesus suffered and He warned His disciples they would suffer (Matt. 10:16–42).

At times God allows a bit of trouble or pain into our lives. He's making warriors of us, not cupcakes. David said, "Blessed be the LORD my strength, which teacheth my hands to war, and my fingers to fight." Did God come down to earth and train David to war with hand-to-hand combat? No, He didn't; He trained him by allowing difficult circumstances and difficult people into his life.

I don't know what troubles God will use to build your faith, or mine, but I do know that if He allows or orchestrates something, there's a reason for it. The things we suffer aren't always for our benefit. Maybe your reaction to your pain or story of deliverance will be the catalyst that pushes someone else into their destiny, or maybe your testimony of victory is what someone needs to hear to believe God will take care of their problem too.

Although God hears your prayers every time you pray, your deliverance may be prolonged. Maybe God hasn't answered you because He wants to teach you something you haven't yet learned. Maybe how to wait on Him is being finetuned or you're being taught to believe Him for the impossible. Maybe it's preparation for something else. David might not have been able to kill Goliath if God had not prepared him through his encounter with the bear and the lion (1 Sam. 17:34–37). Think about this: God didn't prevent the bear and the lion from invading David's space, but he did protect David from being killed by them.

Whether God responds to your prayer quickly or not, or whether He answers it the way you want Him to or not, just know that He does hear you. Believe in God for your breakthrough. Don't worry about what your problem looks like. Looks can be deceiving. I like the examples of Job, Daniel, and his three friends Shadrach, Meshach, and Abednego who trusted God to deliver them though their deaths seemed imminent. Remember that God loves you, and He hears every word you utter or think.

If you don't t know the Lord as your Savior, you have a bigger problem than you may realize. To reject Christ's sacrifice of dying on the Cross for our sins leads to eternal damnation, but this doesn't have to be the case for you; there's an easy fix. Jesus is waiting for a chance to be Your Lord and Savior. If you would like to be in a relationship with Him, pray this prayer with me.

Dear Lord, I am a sinner, but I don't want to be. I believe that You are God's son. I believe that You died on the Cross for my sins and rose again on the third day. Forgive me for all my sins and save me. Thank You, Lord. Amen.

## 14

# GOD IS LARGE AND IN CHARGE

Great is the LORD, and greatly to be praised; and
his greatness is unsearchable.

—Psalm 145:3

In this psalm, David is extolling the greatness of God. I believe verse 3 is a summarization of verses 1–21. God is indeed great and mysterious. It is above our capacity as human beings to figure Him out—how He does what He does or where His power comes from. The *Clarke Commentary* says of the unsearchableness of God: "Literally, To his mightinesses there is no investigation. All in God is unlimited and eternal."

To paraphrase the greatness of God is to say that He is large and in charge. There is nothing impossible for Him to accomplish. If you're worried about anything, including the coronavirus, monkeypox, and polio, stop worrying. God is more powerful than all these things. Regarding the coronavirus, many have died because of it; numerous individuals have also died from cancer and other ailments, but this does not negate the fact that God is still sovereign.

We don't know why the pandemic was allowed to wreak havoc in the world, but God knows. We don't know why He allows any of the sicknesses or tragedies to enter our lives but He knows that too. Somethings we will never know but I do know that He is always in control of what's going on in the world. Sometimes we want to know the secret things of God but we can't even handle what He has given us to know.

It is normal to be concerned about the virus with all the death and pain it has inflicted on so many nations, but worrying about it won't change a thing. Worry is not the answer; Jesus is. God wants you to be careful, observing safety precautions, but He doesn't want you to be afraid of what's going on in the world, whether it be the virus, racial tensions, or problems of a more personal nature. I'm not making light of your difficulties or fears; I'm just reminding you that God is more powerful than anything you may be experiencing.

Psalm 46:1–3 says: "God is our refuge and strength, a very present help in trouble. Therefore will not we fear, though the earth be removed, and though the mountains be carried into the midst of the sea; Though the waters thereof roar and be troubled, though the mountains shake with the swelling thereof. Selah." The events of this psalm sound like an unimaginable earthquake and a flood of gigantic proportions never experienced in our lifetime. Have you ever heard of mountains falling into the sea? I haven't. None of these issues are a problem for God. He can handle earthquakes, floods, tsunamis, and any calamities that may strike the earth and our lives. The psalmist and his peers seem to grasp this concept very well.

Although the psalmist has painted a drastic picture

of devastation, he has made up his mind along with other unnamed voices about how they will react to such catastrophes; *They will not fear*! I admire the psalmist and his friends. They probably wouldn't let me be a member of their group because I still become frightened sometimes when my trouble seems more than I can bear. I can happily say though that even before I got saved, I was never like the person on the television program who had to be slapped to make them stop screaming and to calm down.

Deuteronomy 31:8 says: "And the Lord, he it is that doth go before thee; he will be with thee, he will not fail thee, neither forsake thee: fear not, neither be dismayed." Hebrews 13:5 repeats this same thought. Why does the Bible tell us not to be afraid? Because God knows who we are. Most importantly He knows who he is—God Almighty. That's why He tells us not to fear. Nothing, absolutely nothing, fazes Him because He is large and in charge.

Because of who our Father is we never have to fear anything. God has us covered. Even if we're being attacked there's no need to worry. God's Word says in Isaiah 54:17: "No weapon that is formed against thee shall prosper." If we live long enough weapons will form against us, but when they do, rest assured that God has not left us unarmed. He has given us spiritual weapons. Second Corinthians 10:4–5 says: "For the weapons of our warfare are not carnal, but mighty through God to the pulling down of strongholds; Casting down imaginations, and every high thing that exalteth itself against the knowledge of God, and bringing into captivity every thought to the obedience of Christ." Whatever weapons are formed against us are a blessing in God's hands. He may use those weapons to teach us a spiritual lesson and/or to strengthen us. Whatever the case, Romans 8:31 says: "What shall we then say to these things? If God be for us who can be against us?" Do I need to answer that question for you?

God is our protector, and He wants us to turn to Him when we're in trouble, in pain, or worried about something. He wants to be our refuge, our safety net, the first person we think of when trouble docks at our door. Whatever is bothering you, talk to God about it. I once heard someone say, "I don't tell God all my stuff because I don't want to bother Him." That person doesn't know how deeply God loves us. We could never bother Him by telling Him all about our troubles. He doesn't get tired of hearing from us. He is our Father. We're supposed to come to Him. Who else can we turn to? That stuff that's so big to us isn't big to God at all. That's right; to Him our big stuff is little stuff. He is the LORD God Almighty, the Great I am.

Think about this. He is the same God who created the world ex nihilo (out of nothing). God created not just the earth, but He also created time and space. He created all the planets and galaxies, and the heavens. He spoke into existence day and night, the sun and the sky. He created animals, grass, trees, flowers, and vegetation. He created man, too, in His image. No matter how bad things are for you, God loves you, and He wants to help you. Always remember that He is large and in charge. He always has been, and He always will be.

First Samuel chapter 5 tells the story of the Philistines defeating the Israelites in battle. After their victory over Israel, the Philistines took the Ark of the Covenant from them and placed it in the temple of their chief god, Dagon, in Ashdod. When the Philistines went to the temple the next morning, Dagon had fallen on its face before God. The Philistines picked up their god (he couldn't even get up on his own), and they placed him back where he was before God.

The very next morning, Dagon was fallen on his face again, but this time his head and the palms of his hands were cut off and lying on the threshold of the temple. Not only did God destroy the Philistines' chief god, Dagon, but He destroyed the people of Ashdod and smote the surrounding areas with emerods (archaic word for hemorrhoids). I don't even want to imagine how they suffered. They should never have taken the Ark of the Covenant, a symbol of faith and of God's presence for Israel. It was holy and should have remained with the Israelites. God had also stipulated that the ark was not to be touched by anyone; it was to be carried with staves (Exod. 25:1). It most definitely should not have been placed in the temple of the Philistine god.

What were some others acts of the Bible that showed God's sovereignty? In Numbers 16: 31–33, the Korahites tried to usurp God's authority concerning Aaron as the high priest. God caused the earth to open and swallow Korah, his cohorts, all their families, and their possessions.

He smote the Egyptians with plagues and drowned Pharaoh and his army in the Red Sea. In Daniel chapter 4, Nebuchadnezzar thought it was his power and might that had built Babylon, but he learned who deserved the credit when God took his mind and his majesty for a season. His son, Belshazzar, learned this lesson in the next chapter, more harshly. He was slain and his kingdom given to the Medes because he did not honor God. He did not learn from his father's lesson. In Acts 12:20–23, King Herod was eaten by worms because he did not give God His glory when his audience shouted after his public address, "This is the voice of a god, not a man."

Repeatedly the Bible demonstrates God's sovereignty. There are gods, small g, and there is *God*. He is God of gods; that's who He is. The Philistines believed Dagon was a god. A lot of the ancient nations had their particular gods. The Israelites often fell into depravity and embraced the gods of other nations, but look who's still here after all this time. Isaiah 46:9 says: "Remember the former things of old: for I am God, and there is none else; I am God, and there is none like me."

I find it amazing how some people run behind movie stars, musicians, and athletes not realizing or acknowledging that God Almighty is greater than all these people combined. They can't heal you or deliver you from evil. They definitely can't save your soul from hell; they can't even save themselves, but God can because He's large and in charge. Whatever you need, the Lord can supply it; whatever attack you may be under, He can deliver you from it.

God is in control of everyone and everything. Even if He doesn't do something that you want Him to do, it doesn't mean He can't do it. Don't lose faith in God when He doesn't answer your prayer the way you want Him to or at the time you want Him to. He's not your slave, He's not Santa Claus. He is God! His ways are beyond our comprehension. Although we may not understand why we are suffering or why God is allowing it to continue, He always has a reason for what He does; we just don't know what His reasons are.

Years ago I was having a problem with my front tooth. It was sliding out of the socket. My grandbaby said, "Grandma, your tooth is coming out." I said, "No, baby, it just looks like it is." I had faith, call it childish faith or whatever you want to call it, but I believed that God was going to push that tooth back up in my mouth. During that same period one of my girlfriends came over. She said the same thing my grandson said, and I told her the same thing I told my grandson, "No, it's not coming out; it just looks like it is." I kept praying and believing God for healing and to fix my tooth problem—to push it back up in my mouth where it belonged. Well, wouldn't you know it, one night at work while talking to two coworkers; my tooth slid out of my mouth and hit the floor (while we were talking about Jesus, too).

My girlfriend's eyes got big like Buckwheat's, and we laughed as I scooped the tooth up off the floor. I acted like it didn't bother me, but I was so hurt, because I believed that God was going to heal my mouth, and I wasn't going to lose my tooth. When I got alone with God I said, "God, I need you to tell me something, because I know I had faith that you would heal me." God spoke to me and said, "You don't choose how I heal you." My lesson for that day was that God is in charge of when, where, how, and if He heals me. He's in charge of how He heals you, too.

Even if He takes me home to be with Him, I'm still healed, because there's no sickness in heaven. My job, our job, is to believe God's Word, no matter what situations may arise, and no matter how impossible or faraway our deliverance may seem. Although my tooth did fall out that day, I still believe God could have repaired my tooth enabling me to keep it. That's what I'm supposed to believe, and I do. What about you? Will you believe that God is large and in charge, no matter what?

How wonderful that as high and lofty as He is, God wants to be in a relationship with us. He wants to be our Lord and Savior. Jesus Christ died on the Cross to atone for our sins. Won't you give Him a chance to show you who He is? If your answer is yes, pray this prayer with me.

Heavenly Father, thank You so much for giving Your only Son to die on the Cross for me. I am truly sorry for my sins, and I repent of my sins, asking for Your forgiveness. I acknowledge and accept Your gift of salvation, and because of this, I am now saved. Thank You so much, Lord. In Jesus's name I pray. Amen.

## 15

# NOTHING IS TOO HARD FOR GOD

Ah Lord God! Behold, thou hast made the heaven
and the earth by thy great power and stretched
out arm, and there is nothing too hard for thee.
—Jeremiah 32:17

In this chapter, Nebuchadnezzar, the king of Babylon, and his army seized Jerusalem, taking them into captivity and setting fire to the city and to the houses. The people also suffered famine, pestilence, and the sword because they did none of what the Lord commanded them to do (Jer. 32:23–24). As bad as all this was, God was merciful toward them and told Jeremiah that He would bring His people back to Jerusalem, and they would live there in safety at a later time. Jeremiah probably had doubts about God restoring the people to the land after what he had seen. Did Jeremiah believe his own words from verse 17, that "nothing is too hard for God?" Is that why God said to him, "Behold, I am the LORD, the God of all flesh: is there anything too hard for me" (verse 27)?

In Genesis 18:14, the Lord asked Abraham, "Is anything

too hard for the Lord?" He asked him this question because when his wife, Sarah, overheard the Lord tell Abraham that about that time next year she would have a son, she laughed. Sarah didn't believe what the Lord had said because of her age, but Abraham believed Him. The Bible says he was not weak in faith and did not even consider that his body was dead and so was Sarah's womb (Rom. 4:19). Abraham knew that nothing was too hard for God—not even giving him and Sarah a son in their old age.

The Lord blessed others this way too. Elizabeth, the mother of John the Baptist, became pregnant, though she and her husband, Zacharias, were old. God used Elisha to prophecy the pregnancy of the Shunammite woman. At a later date her son died and was brought back to life. That was God. Hannah, the mother of Samuel, was blessed with six children whereas before she had none. Let's not forget Mary, the mother of Jesus. She wasn't barren; she was a virgin, yet she conceived Jesus Christ, God's Son. Nothing is too hard for the Lord!

One of God's character traits is His omnipotence, which means He's all-powerful. No one anywhere in the entire universe is mightier than He is. Anything you need, no matter how big, small, or complicated, God can do it. It's not too hard for Him to do. What problem are you struggling with? What sickness is wracking your body? What financial issues are plaguing you? Whatever that thing is, talk to God about it. He's always listening, and He can help you.

There are so many instances in the Bible of people being in trouble and God coming to their rescue. He healed many who were sick with all kinds of diseases and ailments, some who had mental problems, people who were possessed with demons, couples who couldn't have children, and people who had no food to eat. There's much more, but you can contemplate for yourself how many times God helped you. If you're reading this sermon, He's granted you another day of life, and that's impressive enough all by itself.

God is so amazing. You can never go wrong depending on Him; Why don't you trust Him with your life today? Accept the more than remarkable gift of His Son, Jesus Christ as your Savior. Don't let Satan trick you into believing the life you now live is as good as it gets. It isn't. Even if you have loads of money, a great big, loving family, and your health is great, there is more to be had—much more. You can't imagine what God has planned for those who accept Christ as their Savior. Are you ready to accept Him as your Lord and Savior? If so, pray this prayer with me.

Heavenly Father, thank You for sending your Son, Jesus, to die on the Cross for me. Please forgive me for all of my sins. I am sorry and repent of them. I accept Your gift of salvation. Thank You so much, Lord. Amen.

# 16

# WHAT DO YOU NEED FROM GOD?

But my God shall supply all your need according
to his riches in glory by Christ Jesus.
—Philippians 4:19–21

I have a question for you today. "What do you need from God?" I'm not asking you what you want. I'm asking you what you need. I don't know what problems or troubles the Philippians were experiencing that prompted Paul to comfort them with the promise that God would meet all of their need in this passage, but I do believe that this very assurance was not only true for the Philippians, but it is also true for you and me today, as well. God will meet our need too.

He owns everything, and He never runs out of anything. Psalm 50:10–12 says: "For every beast of the forest is mine, and the cattle upon a thousand hills. I know all the fowls of the mountains: and the wild beasts of the field are mine. If I were hungry, I would not tell thee: for the world is mine, and the fulness thereof." These verses of scripture aren't about God's ability to take care of anyone. They are about

Him not needing sacrifices from the Israelites, or any of us; however, if one reads these verses carefully, it is clear that God has more than enough of everything because the world belongs to Him. So what do you need?

Our needs and wants are especially important to us, but the two are not of equal value. A need is something you can't live without like food, air, or water. A want is something you can live without, even though you may think you can't or may not want to do without. Many of us, maybe most of us, pray not only for what we need but for things we want as well. I know I do. I believe Zacharias, the father of John the Baptist, did too. What was it he wanted and believed he needed from God? He wanted a child.

Psalm 127:3 says: "Lo, children are an heritage of the LORD; and the fruit of the womb is his reward." Zacharias and his wife, Elizabeth, wanted this reward. Zacharias had prayed so many years for a child that when the angel Gabriel showed up and told him that his prayer would be answered Zacharias, did not believe him. I think of how Zacharias continued to pray year after year for this blessing, and I believe that his desire for a child may have been predicated on what he considered a need more than a want. Zacharias and Elizabeth were very old, and in their lifetime, there was no such thing as Social Security or pension plans. Therefore, it was possible, and it would have been normal, if these elderly parents expected a child to help them with physical and financial support in this stage of their lives.

According to Luke 1:16–17, Gabriel the angel told Zacharias that he would have a son who would be a joy and a delight to him. He also told the priest that the child (John) would be a blessing for the nation of Israel, turning many of them to the Lord their God. All that Gabriel forecast to Zacharias came true. An important lesson we can learn from Zacharias is to never give up when we petition God for something. It doesn't matter how long we've been praying for a particular thing. We should keep praying to Him until we receive what we're praying for or until we get an answer concerning that thing.

In Luke 18:1–8, Jesus tells a parable of the persistent widow. According to verse 1 of this chapter, Jesus's purpose for telling the parable was "to show his disciples that they should always pray and not give up." Let's be as persistent as the widow of the parable was. Moreover, let's be obedient to Jesus Christ and grasp His lesson about praying continuously. Whatever His response to our prayer is, whether it be yea or nay, we should trust Him. He knows what He's doing, and He knows what is best for us.

I must address the fact that many of us have been praying a long time and are still praying for something we feel we need from God. Our prayers may be for healing, financial, and/or emotional help. We wait and wait on God, and some of us feel like He isn't hearing us. If we're waiting, it means we're still alive, and whether we acknowledge it or not, God is hearing us, and He is seeing to our needs. For those things we don't feel He's addressed, maybe He just hasn't done so yet, or maybe He does not see our problems or ailments as the hindrances in our lives that we believe they are.

In Luke 4:25–27, Jesus said there were many widows and many lepers in Israel in the time of Elijah who weren't fed and cured of leprosy, but Elijah was sent only to the widow of Zarephath and to Naaman, a commander of the army of the king of Aram. They both received miracles; she was fed, and Naaman was healed. Although the gist of this passage is not about healing and feeding, it does let us know that not everyone is going to receive the types of miracles the widow of Zarephath and Naaman experienced on this side of life.

No matter how long you've been praying, keep praying and thanking God in advance. We must persist in prayer because it is God's will for us to do so. I've said it before: how and when God responds to our prayers is His business. Our business is to continue asking, seeking, knocking, and believing He will answer us. Galatians 6:9 says not to be weary in well-doing. In this scripture is the promise that if we don't faint, we shall reap a reward at God's proper time. Continuing to pray is considered well-doing.

Another thing worth mentioning about this subject is that if you have needs, and you haven't talked to God about them, you should. Do you shy away from asking God for what you need because you don't believe He can or will answer you? Have you read James 4:2–3, which says: "Ye have not because ye ask not"? James says to his audience, "You do not receive what you're asking for because you are asking amiss, asking for something selfishly." Are you like the people that James is talking to? Are your prayers all about you—all about what you want?

Many of us do our best to pray according to God's will. We pray for ourselves, our families, our friends, our neighbors, for healing from sickness, financial issues, the eradication of the coronavirus, and for the Ukrainians. We pray for people all over the world, and for some of us this includes praying for our enemies, as the Bible says we should. With all this praying going on, there's still so much more we haven't prayed about. The Bible says we don't even know what we should be praying for. Thank God for His Holy Spirit who intercedes on our behalf through wordless groans. He intercedes for God's people by the will of God (Rom. 8:26–27). Aren't you glad we have the Holy Spirit as our prayer intercessor? I certainly am!

In 2 Corinthians 12:9, Paul prayed to God about a problem that the Bible called "a thorn in the flesh." Paul continued to seek God about removing it until God told him His grace was sufficient for him. After God's answer to Paul, he no longer fretted over his "thorn." Just because God told Paul His grace was sufficient for his thorn problem doesn't mean that's your answer for your predicament. Yes, God's grace is sufficient for all of us; however, you are to pray about your situation until you get the answer He has for you.

Jehovah Jireh is one of God's names. It means "our provider." We humans can't fathom just how much God provides for us. Paul's need was relief from a thorn in the flesh. What's yours? In 1 Kings. 17:4–6, Elijah the prophet had a need. Without God's intervention, he was going to die. King Ahab and Queen Jezebel were seeking Elijah to kill him because he had prophesied there would be no rain in the land for years to come. To protect Elijah, God instructed him to hide in the Kerith Ravine. Here Elijah drank water and ate food that God had commanded the ravens to supply him with.

Later the brook dried up, so God sent Elijah to Zarephath. There Elijah met a widow who was gathering sticks for herself and for her son to eat and die. She didn't have enough oil and flour for another meal. Through Elijah, God announced to the widow, "The jar of flour will not be exhausted, and the jug of oil will not run dry until the day the LORD sends rain upon the face of the earth." You're just as important to God as Elijah and the widow of Zarephath were. God supplied their needs, and He'll supply yours too.

God also provided for Joseph, his entire family, and all Egypt during the time of a seven-year famine. As a teenage boy, Joseph had been sold into slavery by his jealous brothers. Later, during this same period, Joseph was incarcerated over a false allegation concerning his master's wife. He was now doubly imprisoned, a slave and an inmate. Nevertheless, God's favor was still mightily upon him. Although Joseph didn't know it, "all things were working for good" (Rom. 8:28). Though originally shackled and imprisoned Joseph was eventually released and promoted to a position of power in Egypt second only to the Pharaoh. Joseph's prominence now surpassed that of the man who had thrown him in jail. Look at God! Joseph and his family's needs were met, and he received the bonus of being released from prison and given a high-ranking title.

During all these years Joseph may not have understood why such trouble had befallen him, but God had a plan for Joseph's life. His purpose was to position Joseph so that when the seven years of famine came to Egypt, Joseph would be able to feed many who would have otherwise starved to death. The twelve tribes of Israel were included in this group of people. When you're experiencing a tough time, and you don't understand what's going on in your life, I pray you will think about Joseph as an example of how God can turn your troubles into blessings and how He's working something out for good even when nothing seems to be going your way. Romans 8:28 was true for Joseph, and it's true for you and me as well.

Although this sermon is mainly about God supplying our needs, many times He gives us our wants too. Psalm 37:4 says: "Delight thyself also in the LORD; and he shall give thee the desires of thine heart." This verse has often been misunderstood. God giving you the desires of your heart doesn't mean He'll give you everything you ask for, although numerous times He does grant us our requests. What this verse means is that as a born-again Christian, the Holy Spirit works in our hearts; He tailors our desires to coincide with God's plans for us. These desires (which you might think are solely yours) often come from God, and He will fulfill them as He sees fit.

My alma mater, Nyack College, is a missions-oriented school. It offers trips all over the world. A couple of years ago while studying for my degree I saw a brochure advertising a trip to Israel. For me to travel to Israel would be a dream come true, because of the biblical and historical value of such a place and because it would fulfill a class requirement for that semester.

This was a wonderful opportunity for me, but I had a problem; I couldn't afford the price tag. So what did I do? I went to my Father and asked Him to provide for me so I could go on the trip. Not long after I prayed about it, overtime on my job opened. This hadn't happened in a long time for the area in which I work. We began to get so much overtime that I just knew this was God answering my prayer. The overtime flowed until I not only had the money for the trip, but I also had money for souvenirs. Another thing God did for me was to give me the strength to do all that overtime while going to school full time and working full time.

I saw and experienced so much in Israel. I was in the Garden of Gethsemane where Jesus spent time praying before He was arrested. I visited Bethlehem and the manger area where Christ was born; I went inside the tomb where He was placed after His death; I sailed on the Sea of Galilee, and I even got to ride a camel. It was wonderful. I came back home with a clearer understanding of where Jesus lived and ministered while walking the earth.

Two years later, in 2018, I was sitting in class and asked the dean (who had dropped in) when the next class on divine healing would take place. Oh, how I wanted to take that class. He said there wouldn't be one this semester on school grounds, but there would be one in Cuba. Well, at first, I didn't want to go to Cuba, but the more I thought about it, the desire to do so began to grow within me. I told God, "I 'think' I want to go to Cuba." I wasn't sure, but I said, "God if you want me to go to Cuba could you make a way for me to go and give me the money for this trip?"

Again, God stepped in and gave me the finances to pay for the trip to Cuba. I received a stipend check from the school, which covered the entire bill. They had taken too much money out for my student loan. Was I worried about paying it back? No, ma'am; no, sir. God provided for me to go to Israel and Cuba, and He is providing for my student loan to be paid. He has always taken care of me, and I know that He always will. God is such a faithful Father, and He knows how to look after His children. "If ye then, being evil, know how to give good gifts unto your children, how much more shall your Father which is in heaven give good things to them that ask Him" (Matt. 7:11). Were those trips to Israel and Cuba my wants or my needs? I think they were both. I have been enriched by both trips, and I am wiser because of them.

I asked the question at the beginning of the sermon, "What do you need from God?" Have you figured it out yet? More than anything, you need Him. John 3:16 says: "For God so loved the world that he gave his only begotten Son, that whosoever believeth in him should not perish, but have everlasting life." God offers us salvation and eternal life. Won't you accept Jesus Christ as your Savior? He'll love you as no one else can and will supply all your needs. If your answer is yes to accepting His love, let us pray.

Dear God, thank You for loving me the way You do. Thank You for supplying all my needs. God, I want to be saved. Forgive me for all the sins I've committed. Cleanse my heart and help me to love You and others according to Your teachings. I accept Your gift of atonement through Jesus Christ, who died on the Cross for me. Thank You, God. Amen.

# 17

# Ain't He Good?

O Taste and see that the LORD is good.
—Psalm 34:8

The subject of today's message is about the goodness of the LORD. For those who've accepted Christ as their Savior, I want to ask you a question about Him: "Ain't He good?" For those who don't yet know Him as their Savior, you too have experienced the goodness of the LORD. Matthew 5:45 says: "He causes his sun to rise on the evil and the good, and sends rain on the righteous and the unrighteous. So in answer to my question, "Ain't He good?" We can all emphatically say, "Yes, He is. He's soooo good."

The Bible is the foremost authority on the LORD's goodness, and it is full of affirmations, stories, and examples of how wonderful He is. We are walking, talking, and breathing examples of the goodness of God. When I think about the LORD—His virtue, His love, His protection, and His compassion toward me—I can't help but thank Him. At times, my heart leaps for joy at the very thought that He loves me so much. He's so good that He even cares for those who don't care for Him. Romans 5:7–8 says: "For scarcely for a righteous man will one die; yet peradventure for a good man some would even dare to die. But God commendeth his love toward us, in that, while we were yet sinners, Christ died for us." So, I ask the question again, "Ain't He good?"

First Chronicles 16:34 says: "O give thanks to the LORD; for he is good; for His mercy endureth forever." Who do you know other than God who can live up to that kind of declaration? He's so good that His mercy toward us started before we were born. It blankets us in the present and reaches into eternity, covering us, loving us with an everlasting love, though we've done absolutely nothing to earn it.

While Jesus walked the earth, He went about teaching, feeding, healing, delivering, and setting people free from sin, sickness, and many other afflictions. After He went back to heaven, He didn't stop thinking about us or looking out for us. He continues to work on our behalf as our mediator, standing between God and our sins. He is preparing a place for us so that we can live with Him eternally. He always has our best interests at heart. "Ain't He good?"

When we pray to Him, He hears us. When we're in trouble He delivers or strengthens us. When we're depressed, He comforts us, and when we're in a bind, "bam!" there He is ready to help us. The LORD has done and is always doing so much for us. The Mississippi Mass Choir recorded the song "I Just Can't Tell It All." I agree with that sentiment. You can't tell all of how good He is; no one can because His goodness is unfathomable.

In Romans 8:35–39, Paul gives a great pericope of how powerful God's love for us is. He describes how nothing, absolutely nothing, can separate us from His love, and as much as Paul knew about God (he wrote more New Testament books than any other apostle), even he couldn't tell it all about the goodness of the LORD. The thing that stands out the most for me is that God sent Christ to become a sacrifice on the Cross for me and because of Him, I will never truly die. "Ain't He good?"

I didn't know what good was until I accepted Christ as my savior. If you're born again, you know what I'm talking about. As I meditate on God's Word, I can imagine Daniel and his friends in a conversation about God asking each other, "Ain't He good?" I can almost hear Joseph, Esther, and Gideon at some point proclaiming the LORD's goodness. I can look backward in time to David, Peter, and Paul and I can also look forward to the future, and I imagine hearing all the saints of God shouting with wild abandon, "*God is good! God is good!*"

David was constantly extolling the goodness of the LORD as we should be in thanks to all He is constantly doing for us. In one instance David said, "I had fainted, Unless I had believed to see the goodness of the LORD in the land of the living." Another time he invites the audience to taste and see how good God is. We'll never find anyone whose goodness compares to His. It just isn't possible. He's just that good.

Today He is giving you a chance to see how good He is. Won't you taste and see? Why reject a gift of unconditional love? Do you really have enough love that you don't need His? Jesus Christ is waiting for you to come to Him. If you're willing and ready for a new life, and to become a new creature in Christ (2 Cor. 5:17), taste and see by praying this prayer with me.

Heavenly Father, thank You for loving me so much that You gave Your only Son to die on the Cross in my place. Dear Savior, I'm sorry for all my sins. Forgive me, Lord. Give me a new heart, a heart bent toward You. Thank You, God, for hearing my prayer and for saving me. In Jesus name I pray. Amen.

# 18

# MY GOD, MY PROVIDER

And Abraham stretched forth his hand, and took
the knife to slay his son. And the angel of the
Lord called unto him out of heaven, and said,
Abraham, Abraham: and he said, Here am I. And
he said, Lay not thine hand upon the lad, neither
do thou anything unto him: for now I know that
thou fearest God, seeing thou hast not withheld
thy son, thine only son from me And Abraham
lifted up his eyes, and looked, and behold behind
him a ram caught in a thicket by his horns: and
Abraham went and took the ram, and offered him
up for a burnt offering in the stead of his son. And
Abraham called the name of that place Jehovah-
Jireh: as it is said to this day, In the mount of the
Lord it shall be seen."

—Genesis 22:10–14

Hallelujah to the King of kings and the Lord of Lords,
who supplies all our needs. God has many names, for He is
so majestic, omnipotent, and awesome that one name won't

cover all of who He is. Jehovah Jireh—Yahweh Yireh, which means the Lord will provide—is today's sermon topic. This passage is about the story of God testing Abraham's faithfulness to see if he would sacrifice his son to Him. We've read the above scriptures about this event and therefore we know that Abraham passed the test.

When I read Genesis 22:14, I was a little surprised that God as Jehovah-jireh wasn't mentioned at the beginning of the book of Genesis since it's where we begin to learn about Him as a provider. As I continued to think about it, I realized the principle of Jehovah-jireh has always been present in His Word whether specifically mentioned or not. For instance, the Lord provided for Adam and Eve while they lived in the Garden of Eden and after they were kicked out of it. Noah and his family had food, shelter, and protection while they were in the ark, during the Flood, and so were all the animals they had gathered. The Deluge destroyed all living creatures on the earth, but the residents of the ark were safe.

Jehovah-jireh provided for Hagar, Abraham's baby's mama, and their son too. Abraham sent them away because of Sarah's jealousy. They wandered in the Desert of Beersheba until they ran out of water. Then the crying started. Hagar was crying, and her son was crying. They didn't cry for long, though. The angel of the Lord appeared to Hagar and while talking to her, Hagar's eyes were opened, and she saw a well of water (Gen. 21:14–19). God had provided for her and her son in the desert.

God always has and always will provide for His children. Most of the time He beats us to the punch and gives us what we need before we ask Him to. Isaiah 65:24 says, "And it shall come to pass, that before they call, I will answer; and while they are yet speaking, I will hear." Did you ask God to wake you up this morning? Did you ask for the air you breathe? Matthew 6:25–34 says He knows what we need, and He'll give it to us. He'll provide for us just as He does for the birds mentioned in this passage.

In 2 Kings chapter 4, God provided for a widow whose two sons were about to be taken as servants for a creditor. Her deceased husband had incurred debt with the man and the creditor wanted the debt settled. The widow couldn't stop the creditor from seizing her sons because she had no money. All she had was one jar of oil in the house. Elisha instructed her to borrow jars from all her neighbors and to pour the oil into those jars. She did as she was told and the oil kept flowing until there were no more containers to pour oil into. Elisha then told her to sell the oil to pay the creditor and to live on the rest of it. That was God's provision (2 Kings 4:1-7).

In another instance, Jesus fed over five thousand people in Matthew 14, and over four thousand more in the next chapter. Again, that was God as Provider. Paul said in Philippians 4:19: "But my God shall supply all your need according to his riches in glory by Christ Jesus." Never doubt God's provision. He owns everything, and He can provide for you.

On a more personal level, God has taken care of me repeatedly. Once many years ago after getting paid and paying my bills there was nothing left over for me. I told God I didn't have any money for myself for the next two weeks, and I felt like crying. I reminded Him (as if He didn't know) that I paid my tithes and gave my offerings. I told

Him what His Word from Malachi 3:10 said about bringing all the tithes into the storehouse and proving that He would "open the windows of heaven, and pour me out a blessing, that there shall not be room enough to receive."

During the coming week I received a letter from Con Edison stating that since I continually paid my bill on time, they were refunding my deposit of $100. That was funny to me, amazing too, because I rarely paid that bill on time. More times than not I would only pay Con Ed if they threatened to turn off my lights. The silliness of it was that I had the money to pay them. I can truthfully say today that I have matured concerning my finances. Instead of holding on to the money allotted for bills, I pay them as they come in.

I think this act falls into the category of being faithful over a few things, a lesson from Matthew 25:23. After all, paying my bills on time is another way of treating others the way I would like to be treated. If someone owed me money for a service I rendered, would I like it if they just held on to the money because it didn't affect their credit report? That's what I was doing. It doesn't matter if it's a person or a business. If you owe money, whether to a company or a person, you should pay them. We should always do right by others when possible.

Throughout the sermon, we've heard of many instances of God providing for His children. I would like to mention the most important provision He has ever made for us. John 3:16 says: "For God so loved the world, that he gave his only begotten Son, that whosoever believeth in him should not perish, but have everlasting life." Through Jesus Christ the Father has provided a way for us to live eternally with Him after our life on this earth is done. Jesus Christ died on the Cross in our place to atone for our sins. He did the hard part. Our part is to accept His gift of salvation. Will you refuse such a wonderful gift? Do you prefer eternity in hell or eternity in heaven with God? The Bible teaches that we will all live again, but the question is where will we live? To seal your destiny, guaranteeing God's perfect future for you with Him, pray this prayer of salvation with me.

Dear God, I am a sinner, and I'm tired of living this way. Please come into my life and be my Savior. I am sorry for all of my sins. Forgive me and grant me new life in You. Thank You, Lord. In the blessed name of Jesus, I pray. Amen.

If you've prayed for Jesus Christ to save you, rejoice. The angels in heaven are rejoicing with you (Luke 15:10). Hallelujah!

# 19

## CHOOSING YOUR WORDS WISELY

(Let's Stop Chopping People Up with Our Words)

For in many things we offend all. If any man offend not in word, the same is a perfect man, and able also to bridle the whole body. Behold, we put bits in the horses' mouths, that they may obey us; and we turn about their whole body. Behold also the ships, which though they be so great, and are driven of fierce winds, yet are they turned about with a very small helm, whithersoever the governor listeth. Even so the tongue is a little member, and boasteth great things. Behold, how great a matter a little fire kindleth! And the tongue is a fire, a world of iniquity: so is the tongue among our members, that it defileth the whole body, and setteth on fire the course of nature; and it is set on fire of hell. For every kind of beasts, and of birds, and of serpents, and of things in the sea, is tamed, and hath been tamed of mankind: But the tongue can no man

> tame; it is an unruly evil, full of deadly poison.
> Therewith bless we God, even the Father; and
> therewith curse we men, which are made after
> the similitude of God. Out of the same mouth
> proceedeth blessing and cursing. My brethren,
> these things ought not so to be.
>
> —James 3:2–10

Have you ever heard the phrase, "Sticks and stones may break my bones, but words will never hurt me?" If you have heard this popular phrase, you know now, or you'll know later that it isn't true because some words do hurt. I once heard someone say words don't hurt them, and if that's true, I say good for them. I don't know anyone whose never been hurt by words at some point in time. The pain of words can come in so many different ways. Some ways include criticism, anger, gossip, lying, etc.

The Bible has a lot to say about words or the tongue. Proverbs 12:18 says: "Reckless words pierce like a sword, but the tongue of the wise brings healing. Another verse, in Proverbs 18:21, says: "Death and life are in the power of the tongue: and they that love it shall eat the fruit thereof." Ummmm, that's a thought; a choice to eat something we've said. Can you eat the fruit of your lips? What do your words taste like daily?

I would like to say I never say wrong or hurtful things, but unfortunately, I would be lying. I can't. There have been times when I've said things that I should not have said or did not say things I should have said. But thank God for Jesus, for He is a forgiver of all our sins, including the ones we commit with our words, like when we talk too much or use profanity, when we lie or gossip about someone. I believe if we could just picture some of the words coming out of our mouths, we would be more careful of what we say to others and ourselves as well.

Words can vilify or they can edify. Some people have been so hurt by words at an early age that they are stuck in a pool of low self-esteem with seemingly no way out. There are others who have always been affirmed and built up, and because of this they believe there is nothing they can't accomplish. A popular phrase is, "If you don't have something good to say about someone, don't say anything." Wouldn't it be great if everyone followed that advice. Whether we are Christians or not, we need to learn how to tame our tongues. We can learn to speak more positively rather than speaking negative, hurtful words to others or ourselves.

James says in chapter 3 that the tongue is a hard thing to tame, and it is, but it's not impossible. When Jesus went back to heaven, He sent us the Holy Spirit to teach us the ways of salvation. We need to acknowledge Him and ask Him to help us with all the things we struggle with in our quest to live holy. This includes helping us to tame our tongues.

Another thing about the tongue and our choice of words is that sometimes we are not aware of the way we talk to others, even if it's meant to be positive. For example, have you ever heard someone say, "I love her to death," or "I love him to death?" Those are not good choices to describe how you feel about someone. There are better ways to express the depth of one's love.

Do you know one of the most important reasons we should tame our tongues? Jesus said we are the light of the world. That means our conversation should reflect light. It means we should shine light into someone's world, and if possible, leave them better than we found them. Words can be a healing balm for some. That's why we should be careful of what we say. Do your words do that? To paraphrase James 3:2, he says that "If a man can tame his tongue, he is perfect, and is able to control his whole body." Is that you? Can you discipline your tongue to never say the wrong thing? I'm not there, but I'm working on it, and the good thing is I have help. The Bible says: "I can do all things through Christ who strengthens me." He's perfect and He wants to perfect you and me. That can only take place if we ask for and accept His gift of salvation. Pray with me.

Heavenly Father, I come to You in the name of Jesus asking for salvation. I am a sinner, but I want to be cleansed from all my unrighteousness. Save me, Lord; forgive me for all my sins. According to Your Word, I am now saved and I thank You. Amen.

## 20

## WORRYING IS WORRISOME

Casting all your care upon him,
for he careth for you.

—1 Peter 5:7

Do you find yourself worrying more than you used to? Were you once a happy-go-lucky person but it seems like "happy" has skipped town and that lucky feeling you once had is now just a memory? The coronavirus pandemic changed the lives of many. The virus continues to mutate and people are still being infected with the different strands of it. Racism is running rampart, and I don't know if the shootings we hear about daily have outpaced the hatred we see in our societies. Numerous individuals are suffering emotionally, economically, socially, and physically. Closer to home, there are those who are grief-stricken, having lost loved ones, friends, coworkers, or neighbors. Worrying is understandable. Life as we knew it a couple of years ago, and before and during the coronavirus has changed drastically.

Some people are worrywarts by nature. They have always worried about this or that, but now because of the virus I suspect there are lots more worriers than there once were. I have never read a scripture that said, "She worried about so and so, or he was worried and upset about this or that," but believe me, people in ancient days worried too. Many of the individuals we read about in the Bible were worried about their problems, not knowing when or if their situations would change for the better. Jesus taught that we shouldn't worry. He asked the question in Matthew 6:27 (paraphrasing), "What can you add to your life by worrying?" In the next chapter, Jesus tells us God will hear our prayers and answer them. Peter knew about worry too. His answer to it was the above scripture at the beginning of the sermon, "Cast all your anxiety on him because he cares for you" (1 Pet. 5:7 (NIV).

Alcohol, drugs (illicit and legal), suicide, and gambling have been around for many years, but because of the pandemic and other societal problems, there seems to be an increase in the number of people who are using some of the above-mentioned vices to cope and relieve their stress. I've noticed that there are more commercials advertising alcohol and gambling than there were a couple of years ago. The reality is that all these things are poor substitutes for true relief from what ails you.

Someone may be asking, "If these things are not the answer for true relief from worries, then what is?" I'm glad you asked that question. Whatever is going on in your life, be it the coronavirus or some other problem, the Bible says (paraphrasing) to cast all your care on the Lord. Our heavenly Father loves you and wants you to come to Him concerning any problem you may have. He wants you to trust Him with the thing that's bothering you.

Through my relationship with the Lord, I have found that He is a problem-solver and worry eraser, and if you allow Him to do so in your life you will experience this fact for yourself.

I remember one time God told me to give Him my rope. He sent someone to me with that message over twenty years ago, and although I can't remember her name, I can remember the impact of what God was saying to me. No, I haven't changed the subject. The rope I'm talking about was my pain and my worries. I was struggling emotionally.

In God's message for me to give Him my rope, I was presented with a picture in my mind of one of my daughters coming to me with a knotted jump rope, asking me to untangle it for her. Before she could even open her mouth, I knew what she wanted, and I was mentally working on the knot. In God's message to me, He was letting me know that as important as untangling my daughters' rope was to me, eradicating my worries was more important to Him. That day I gave Him the rope; I cast my cares on Him, and I still remember the peace I felt afterward.

You see, untangling ropes (solving problems) is easy for God. I wish I could say I never worried after that day, but I'd be lying. At times I've had to remind myself that God can handle any problem I may have. There's no need for me to worry about anything. There's no need for you to worry either. Growing in faith is a process, but with each trial or bit of trouble, I get better at not worrying. I take many things in life as lessons. Sometimes there's something God wants us to learn through our pain. Oftentimes, my experiences have taught me that God always has my back.

Our worries are usually based on the events surrounding

problems we have, but other times not so much. Sometimes, maybe most of the time, our worries are conjectures of things that we think or imagine might happen. Winston Churchill once said. "When I look back on all these worries, I remember the story of the old man who said on his deathbed that he had had a lot of trouble in his life, most of which had never happened." That old man and I had taken a trip on the same boat, worrying about things that might happen but never did. What a waste of time!

Are you a worrier? I would never say it's easy to not worry about problems, but I want to remind you that Jesus said not to worry. Robert S. Eliot once said about worry, "Rule number one is, don't sweat the small stuff. Rule number two is, it's all small stuff." To God, any problem you have is small stuff to Him, so stop your worrying and "cast all your care on God!"

In Matthew 8:24–26, Jesus was asleep on a ship with His disciples when a storm arose. The storm was so violent that it frightened the men, and they woke Jesus up asking Him, "Do you not care that we are perishing?" He in turn asked them a question. "Why are ye fearful, O ye of little faith?" Whatever you're going through, trust the Lord! Why should you trust Him? Because He is God (John 1:1) and because He loves us (John 3:16). You might as well make it a practice to trust Him because worrying changes nothing. I use the word *practice* because that's how we learn most of the time. Practice doesn't always make perfect, as the saying goes, but it does make better.

We're living in difficult times, but it's not as bad as it was for Noah and his family during the Flood. Why do I believe that? I believe it because during the Flood only those eight humans in the Ark survived. The animals living on land were wiped out too; Genesis chapters 6–9 recount the story about it. God told Noah in Genesis 7:4: "Seven days from now I will send rain on the earth for forty days and forty nights, and I will wipe from the face of the earth every living creature I have made."

The Flood is a reminder for me that no matter what's going on in the world, God is still in control. The Bible says the Flood was God's doing. One verse I lean on when I don't understand what's happening in my life or the world is Phil. 4:6-7 (NIV) which states, "Do not be anxious about anything, but in every situation, by prayer and petition, with thanksgiving, present your requests to God. And the peace of God, which transcends all understanding, will guard your hearts and your minds in Christ Jesus." In a nutshell this verse means we shouldn't worry but we should pray about our concerns.

Jesus said in Matthew 6:25–27 that we shouldn't worry about anything—not about what we should eat, drink, or wear, and we shouldn't worry about our bodies. These aren't my words telling you not to worry. These are the words of Jesus Christ who spoke what the Father gave Him to say (John 12:49). God isn't worried about anything and He doesn't want you to worry. He hasn't lost His powers. He's still feeding us, protecting us, healing all types of diseases and ailments, and so much more.

In all we go through, God is with us. He loves us and wants what's best for us. In case you haven't figured out yet what's best for you, it is a relationship with God the Father, God the Son, and God the Holy Spirit. We all need a Savior, and God the Father sent His Son, Jesus Christ, to die on the Cross, shedding His blood for the remission of our sins. Invite Him into your heart. He'll hear you, and He will answer yes to your request for salvation. If you have no idea how to ask Him, just say this prayer.

Lord, I want to be saved. I know there is something deeper and more meaningful than what I've experienced thus far in my life. I want to know You and to change the way I live and think. I want a fresh start. Save me, Lord, forgive me of my sins. Thank You, Lord. I believe You heard me and answered my prayer. Amen.

## 21

# GOD OF THE IMPOSSIBLE

And again I say unto you, It is easier for a camel
to go through the eye of a needle, than for a rich
man to enter into the kingdom of God. When his
disciples heard it, they were exceedingly amazed,
saying, Who then can be saved? But Jesus beheld
them, and said unto them, With men this is
impossible, but with God all things are possible.
—Matthew 19:24–26

My focus for this sermon is Matthew 19:26, in which
Jesus declares, "With God all things are possible." The
disciples were amazed at the possibility of a camel going
through the eye of a needle. They couldn't have imagined
all the other things God would do through Jesus Christ.
Have you ever thought about God's omnipotence and that
nothing is impossible for Him to do? In the three and a half
years of Jesus's ministry He performed many miracles. John
spoke of Him saying, "And there are also many other things
which Jesus did, the which, if they should be written every
one, I suppose that even the whole world would not have

room for the books that would be written" (John 21:25). Jesus did not do ministry alone. The Father was with Him.

Look at the impossibility of a virgin giving birth to a child. Mary did just that, fulfilling the prophecy of the angel Gabriel. Consider how God directed one star among millions to lead the wise men to where the baby Jesus lay. Think about that star and millions of other ones that remained in place because highlighting Jesus' birthplace was not their assignment. Reflect on how vast the universe is. What magnificence! Even before Jesus came to live on the earth, God was excelling at doing the impossible.

When the first test-tube baby was born in the '70s my supervisor at that time said, "Man accomplished something just as God did in making that baby." I disagreed with her stating, "Man had to use material God already created." That conversation ended quickly. No matter how remarkable man is, he is the creation of God. The creation could never outdo the Creator. Man can't even dream big enough to match all of what God has done (Eph. 3:20). God is God and as Jesus said, "With Him all things are possible."

Let's explore an impossibility that wasn't impossible at all—for God. In Joshua 6, God had a novel idea about conquering Jericho. He told Joshua and the army of Israel to march around the wall of the city once each day for six days. The army was to be followed by the armed guards, seven priests blowing trumpets, the ark of the covenant, and lastly, the rear guard. After the army did as they were instructed by Joshua, they had to march around the wall one more time blasting trumpets and making a war cry. On that last day of the final march, day seven, the wall of Jericho collapsed, and the army conquered the city.

The Israelite army destroyed every living thing in Jericho except for Rahab and her family. Rahab had protected the men who came to spy on the city, and in doing so she obtained protection for herself and for her family on the day the army attacked them. The wall of Jericho collapsing was a miracle, and here's another one: Rahab's house was part of that wall (Josh. 2:15) but it was not affected by the march around it. The wall did not fall but was destroyed by the army only after Rahab and her family were safely removed from Jericho (Josh. 6:23–24).

Four chapters later, in Joshua 10:12–13, another seemingly impossible event took place. The Israelites were in battle with the Amorites. Joshua, the leader of the Israelites, was determined to annihilate their enemies, so he prayed to God for the sun to remain still over Gibeon and for the moon to stay over Aijalon until they had defeated them. God honored Joshua's request. The sun remained in the sky seemingly forgetting it was supposed to get out of the way and give place to the moon. It stayed hanging over Gibeon for a full day, and the moon froze in its place over the Valley of Aijalon until the enemies of the Israelites were conquered. This miracle in the sky was easy for God because He can do the impossible.

In another story in the Bible, Shadrach, Meshach, and Abednego, three Hebrew boys, were cast into a fiery furnace. The furnace was so hot that the soldiers who threw them into the blazing structure were killed by the flames licking out of it. The young men were thrown into the fire as punishment for refusing to worship King Nebuchadnezzar's golden statue. Shadrach, Meshach, and Abednego went tumbling into the furnace, but were not hurt. The Bible says: "their hair wasn't singed, their clothes weren't scorched, and they didn't smell of smoke."

King Nebuchadnezzar, who had ordered them thrown into the fire, was amazed because although he knew that three young men had been thrown into the fire, now he saw four men "walking around in it." He also noticed and made a comment that the fourth one looked "like a son of the gods." I'll bet he was also astounded at how they didn't get burned and how they could stroll around in the furnace as if they didn't have a care in the world. This summary of events about the Hebrew boys and the fiery furnace seems impossible too, and it was for man, but not for God (Dan. 3).

Other impossible actions performed by God included making water flow twice from a rock to quench the Israelites' thirst, when they were in the desert (Exod. 17 and Num. 20). This wasn't a little bit of water either. God satisfied the thirst of thousands of people. There were more impossibilities in the Bible that included using water: God instructed Elijah to offer Him a sacrifice of a bullock to prove to the wayward Israelites that He is God. He told Elijah to pour water on the animal, and on the wood that was to burn the sacrifice. He soaked the wood and the bullock with water three times. It was so much water that it ran into the trench surrounding the altar. God sent fire, which consumed not only the sacrifice but also the wood, the stones, the dust, and the excess water in the trench (1 Kings 18:31–38). In the New Testament Jesus walked on water and turned water into wine.

I believe that God's omnipotence over everyone and everything is one of the main points of the lessons Jesus taught. Everything He did—the healings from all manner of sickness and disease, deliverance from demons, raising people from the dead, making the mute talk, the blind see, and the many other miracles He performed while on earth—all point to God the Father and His mastery over impossible situations.

In the book of Luke, Jesus performed at least nineteen miracles. In chapter 5:4–7, He told the fishermen to let down their nets. The men were skeptical because the previous night they had fished and caught nothing. When they obeyed Jesus and let down their nets again, they caught so many fish that the large haul broke their nets. They called for their partners in another ship to come to their assistance, and because they caught such a vast number of fish, both boats began to sink.

God worked all these miracles through Jesus Christ, who gave God the Father the credit for Him being able to work them. In John 5:19, Jesus said: "Verily, verily I say unto you, The Son can do nothing of himself, but what he seeth the Father do: for what things soever he doth, these also doeth the Son likewise." A few verses down, Christ reiterated this statement saying again that He could do nothing apart from the Father (John 5:30).

This sermon is about God's omnipotence—that nothing is impossible for Him to do. I should say there is one thing He won't do whether impossible or not. He won't force you to have a relationship with Him. He loves you and wants you to willingly come to Him. Whether we know it or not, we all need a Savior; we need Him and John 14:6 says we must come to the Father through Jesus Christ. It's the only way. If you want a fresh start, to become a new creature in Christ, and to have all your sins forgiven, you must acknowledge that you believe Jesus Christ is God's Son and that He died for you. Invite Him into your life. If you're ready, pray this prayer with me.

Dear Lord, I am a sinner, but I want to become a new person in You. Thank You for hearing my prayer. Forgive me for all my sins. Thank You for loving me the way You do and for sending Your Son to die on the Cross for me. Thank You so much for saving me. In Jesus's mighty name I pray. Amen.

## 22

# LORD, I DON'T MIND
# A LITTLE SPIT

When he had thus spoken, he spat on the ground,
and made clay of the spittle, and he anointed the
eyes of the blind man with the clay, and said unto
him, Go, wash in the pool of Siloam, (which is by
interpretation, Sent.) He went his way therefore,
and washed, and came seeing.

—John 9:6

The blind man of this passage was healed when Jesus mixed spit with clay and applied it to his eyes. The Bible also mentions Jesus using spit to heal two other men, in Mark 7:31–37, and Mark 8:24. In these passages, one of the men was blind, and the other one was deaf. In all three instances, the men were healed, and whatever they may have thought about spit before they could see, speak, and hear, I believe they now saw it in a different light, since Jesus used it in their healing process.

What is it about spit that makes some people think "Yuck" if it's not their own? Have you ever excused yourself and walked away in disgust from someone who sprinkled droplets of saliva on you while talking (even before COVID)? I noticed in the stories of the three men Jesus healed that not one of them complained about Jesus using His spit to do so. These men were not like Naaman, an Aram army commander who complained about the dirty water of the Jordan River. Elijah had sent him there to wash in it seven times and be healed from leprosy (2 Kings 5:10-14). I wonder if Naaman would have reacted more favorably to a little spit for his healing instead of water from the Jordan River.

Luke 16:19–31 tells of Lazarus the beggar who desired the crumbs from the rich man's table. Verse 21 gave attention to dogs that licked his sores. I've often contemplated why this fact was included in this passage. Is it possible that the dogs licked Lazarus's sores as a sign that they felt compassion for him, or did their spit have healing properties and was therefore a blessing in disguise? *Pubmed* says human spittle has healing qualities in the oral cavity, but there is no mention in this study about the saliva of dogs or any other animals having healing properties. Maybe the dogs felt some sort of empathy for Lazarus; after all, they could have bit him instead of licking his sores.

Spit can be used positively or negatively. When Jesus healed the blind men and the deaf-mute, they were positive actions. I remember as a little girl seeing mothers use spit to clean something on their child's face more than once. Those were positive actions too, even if the grimaces on the children's faces reflected that they felt otherwise. A negative action was the soldiers spitting on Christ while mocking Him. They spit on Him as a sign of disrespect and humiliation (Matt. 26:67). Another negative use of spit comes from the spitting cobra. It spits venom at its enemy's eyes to defend itself, and a camel uses spit as a most unpleasant way of saying, "Get away from me!"

The thought of coming into contact with someone else's spit might make us cringe mentally if not physically, but if we could see it in the light of God's design of our bodies, we might feel differently about it. God created saliva as an important lubricant for our bodily functions. The enzymes in saliva aid in the digestion of our food. It also lubricates our mouths and keeps our lips moist. Imagine if you were eating, and you didn't have saliva in your mouth, especially if there's also no water or juice readily available. You'd have a hard time swallowing your food. What about kissing your mate if you both have dry mouth (Xerostomia), ugh, and who enjoys kissing someone whose lips are cracked and scratchy?

Today the Lord doesn't heal with spit, but if He did, I'd be one of the first ones in line to get a portion of it from Him. I'd even stand proxy for others who are ill and aren't able to be present themselves. No, I wouldn't mind a little of the Lord's spit at all. When Jesus came to earth, He came to do more than heal our physical bodies. He came to heal our sin-sick souls too. He doesn't use spit for this purpose, He shed His blood on the Cross to atone for our sins, and the blood never loses its power. Have you accepted Christ as your Savior? If not, you can be saved today—this very minute. Accept Jesus Christ as your Lord and Savior before it's too late. Pray this prayer with me.

Dear Lord, I'm sorry for my sins. Please forgive me and grant me Your salvation. Thank You, Lord, for hearing my prayer and for saving me. Amen.

## 23

# I'm in Love

Have you ever been in love? I mean deeply in love? I met someone a little over twenty-three years ago, and I just love him. I can't help but love him because he's so wonderful to me. He treats me better than I treat myself, and he shows me how much he loves me every single day. I'm stuck on him, and no one could ever take his place because no one compares to him. No one loves me the way he does, and what I find amazing is that he loved me before I ever loved him, before I even thought about him.

Daily he helps me to become a better person, and not only that, but he is also an excellent provider. He clothes me, he protects me, he feeds me, and he always makes me feel special. He treats me like I'm the only one for him. He is never too busy to listen to my concerns, and he has never, ever ignored me. He doesn't get tired of me talking to him about the same old things over and over. He has never said to me, "I've heard that before," or, "Give it a rest!" When I'm irritated or depressed, he helps me to get through those times.

He doesn't cheat on me; he doesn't lie to me, and he's not a tit-for-tat person. That means he doesn't try to even the score or pay me back for something I've done to hurt or disappoint him. I can get in contact with him anytime, day or night. He has never turned his back on me, even when I turned my back on him. Once when I was young and dumb, I tried to leave him, (I'll never do that again)! He pulled me back to him, loving me as I had never been loved before, loving me as if I had never done anything wrong. Sometimes it's hard to understand how he can love me the way he does.

With him, every day is Valentine's Day. He's never been mean to me in all these years I've been with him, and he's never made me feel small or weak. Those times when I felt alone, I wasn't. He was always there with me. I am comfortable and secure in his love for me because I know that he will never leave me for someone else, and no one can take him from me. That's right; nothing and no one can put a wedge between our love.

Do you have an idea who my love is? His name is Jesus Christ. He is God, He is the Son of God, and He loves me. His love for me cannot be compared to any other love I've ever known, and it is not an exclusive love. He doesn't just love me; He loves you too. John 3:16 says: "For God so loved the world that he gave his only begotten Son, that whosoever believeth in him should not perish, but have everlasting life." I'm not jealous or mad about Him loving you or anybody else for that matter because there's more than enough of Him to go around. He died once, but He loves me so much that death couldn't stop Him from coming back to me. I'm not talking about make-believe, zombie stuff. I'm talking about an authentic resurrection. He came back from the dead and not just for me, but for you too. Because He lives, we shall live also, that is if you accept Him as your Savior.

He wants to be your Lord and Savior. He wants to be in a relationship with you. He won't beg you to give Him a chance. That's a choice you'll have to make for yourself. Some people think that God is so good that He won't send anyone to hell. This is true. He won't. The person who rejects Him is making the choice to go to Hell. God sent His Son to earth to open the way for man to be reconciled to Him through His death on the Cross. The Bible says Jesus Christ is the only way to the Father (John 14:6). If you reject Jesus Christ, you're rejecting the Father.

Have you ever been loved the way I've just described? Jesus offers a love that supersedes anything you've ever experienced. Won't you choose Him today? By accepting His salvation, you will spend eternity with Him in heaven. Are you ready for a fresh start in life? Ask God to forgive you of all your sins. Ask Him to become your Savior. If you do, you'll belong to Him, and when Christ comes back for His church (the believers) you'll be included in the group He whisks away to be with Him forever. Amen! Amen!

## 24

# WHOSE VOICE ARE YOU LISTENING TO?

But he answered and said, It is written, Man shall
not live by bread alone, but by every word that
proceedeth out of the mouth of God.
—Matthew 4:4

This scripture was Jesus's answer to Satan when he tempted Him in the wilderness, and it is also His answer for us today. I'm compelled to ask this question: whose voice are you listening to? Has anyone ever asked you that before? Have you ever thought about which voices are most important to you? We were all created to live by God's Word and not by bread alone. How can we live by His Word, though, if we don't know it, and how can we hear from Him if we're not listening for Him or to Him? Are you listening for His voice? When you pray, do you listen, or do you do all the talking? Do you know that sitting quietly and anticipating a word from God is praying too? Some people believe God doesn't speak audibly. For me, that just means they've never heard Him speak.

Unfortunately, countless people listen to or put more stock in what man says than in what God says. The Bible is full of the Lord's promises to us, but there are those who don't believe His promises are true. A very popular scripture of the Bible states that Jesus is coming back. Revelation 1:7 says: "Behold, he cometh with clouds; and every eye shall see him, and they also which pierced him; and all kindreds of the earth shall wail because of him. Do we believe this verse wholeheartedly? Some of us do, and others do not.

Romans 8:28 states, "And we know that all things work together for good to them that love God, to them who are the called according to *his* purpose." Do we believe it, even when things are painful and/or difficult? Once I was having a conversation with Orease Bowers, one of the most positive people I know. He and I was speaking about Romans 8:28 and I mentioned how I often wondered why God allowed so many troubling things to happen in my life. Orease said, "Those things aren't happening to you, they're happening for you. That statement opened my eyes to see that my concept of that verse was much too shallow. After all, how will I grow and mature if I never go through anything.

In fact, one of my friends, Rogelio Douglas, who is a Bible scholar, told me that the scripture Romans 8:28 (NIV) doesn't say it's working for our good but for the good. He explained that the good is God's plan of salvation and the end time. He said what we go through may not feel good, we may suffer. God's plan may include us sacrificing our life to save others. He also said that ultimately it will be beneficial for us because we'll be with God.

I asked this question at the beginning of the sermon, but I must ask it again: Whose voice are you listening to? This question is of the utmost importance whether you know it or not because listening to God will impact your life like the words no human being ever has or ever will. God loves us. He's concerned about us, and He is continually speaking to us. He speaks to us through His loving-kindness. He speaks to us through His Word, through the visible and even through the invisible things of Him (Rom. 1:20). Some have even heard Him speak audibly.

Many people, surprisingly some of them Christians, do not read their Bibles, but they should. Why? Because in its pages are the truth of God's love for us and His desire to have a relationship with us. The Bible teaches us how to live, how to love, and how to please the Lord. It contains a message from our Creator to us, which if accepted and applied leads to the salvation of our souls. There's a lot of information packed in the sixty-six books of the Bible, and for those who aren't aware of the importance of the Old Testament, it's God's Word too. We need to read, listen to, and study the Bible because there are lots of voices whispering and sometimes screaming into our ears daily.

We need to be careful about which of those voices we give our utmost attention to. This is especially true when seeking advice about some matter of importance. The Bible has lots of examples of individuals who were given good advice and took heed to it thereby acquiring great blessings. There are also instances of those who unwisely listened to bad advice and suffered the consequences.

One person who received good advice and acted on it was Bathsheba, Solomon's mother. She followed the instructions of Nathan the prophet, who told her to remind King David of his promise to her to make Solomon king after him. By listening to Nathan, Bathsheba saved her life and the life of her son (1 Kings 1:11–21). Queen Esther is another person who listened to good advice and because of it saved the lives of all the Jews living in the provinces of Persia. Her uncle Mordecai had prompted her to speak to King Ahasuerus about Haman, his lead administrator, because Haman planned to annihilate all the Jews of the Persian provinces. With the king's permission, Esther concocted a plan of her own and turned the tables on Haman. Instead of the Jews being killed, Haman, his ten sons, and all their enemies in Persia were killed (Esther 7–9).

I have my own story about my life being saved by listening to God. A couple of years ago I was coming home from work, and while driving on the Belt Parkway, I saw this black car exiting on my right at an extremely fast pace. I knew that if I didn't get out of the way, it would smack into me and push me into ongoing traffic. I quickly looked through my left side-view mirror and saw that I couldn't do anything because the cars were whizzing by, and there was no open space for me to enter. I said to God with urgency, "I don't know what to do!" I heard Him say quickly, "Move to your left." I had no time to think; I did what He said, and as soon as I obeyed Him, the black car slammed into the space I had just vacated. God had made an opening for me just in time to move into oncoming traffic. I thought about it later how God gave me the confidence to move over without rechecking to see if I could (there was no time). He saved my life, and I'm so grateful. That was an example of listening to good advice.

These stories are perfect instances of what can happen if good advice is heeded. On the other hand, listening to the wrong advice can get you into a world of trouble, and sometimes killed. Here is one such story. Second Samuel 13:1–29 tells the story of Amnon, one of David's sons who was obsessed with his half sister Tamar. Amnon's first cousin, Jonadab, instructed him on how to trick his half sister into coming to his bedroom so he could have his way with her. This advice coupled with his actions got Amnon killed. Rehoboam, his nephew, also followed wrong advice, although he was first given sound advice for ruling the kingdom. His downfall came because he listened to his friends he grew up with. He rejected the counsel of the old men who had guided his father during his reign as king. Because Rehoboam took the advice of his buddies, all the tribes of Israel except Judah deserted him (1 Kings 12:3–20).

Whose voice are you listening to? Proverbs 3:5–6 says: "Trust in the Lord with all thine heart; And lean not unto thine own understanding. In all thy ways acknowledge him, and he shall direct thy paths." Whatever your needs may be or whatever questions you may have—seek God about them first. He has all the answers. Psalm 32:8 says of God: "I will instruct thee and teach thee in the way which thou shalt go: I will guide thee with mine eye."

If you have asked God for something, wait on Him. He may answer it Himself, or He may give you the answer through someone else. You may feel a pulling or leaning toward what you should do, and you know it's not you. You may not feel anything at all, but because you acknowledged Him, He will help you. He may answer quickly or not so quickly. Whatever the case, God won't steer you wrong. Listen for His voice.

As you continue to mature in Christ and study, (not

just read but study) His Word, you will become more able to distinguish His voice. In John 10:27–28 Jesus said, "My sheep hear my voice, and I know them, and they follow me." Revelation 3:20 says: "Behold, I stand at the door, and knock: if any man hear my voice, and open the door, I will come in to him, and will sup with him, and he with me." Open the door of your heart and listen to His voice. He is calling you. He wants to forgive you of your sins and become your Savior. Listen and let the Lord come in. Amen.

## 25

# DON'T FREAK OUT

Beloved, think it not strange concerning the fiery
trial which is to try you, as though some strange
thing happened unto you: But rejoice, inasmuch
as ye are partakers of Christ's sufferings; that,
when his glory shall be revealed, ye may be glad
also with exceeding joy.
—1 Peter 4:12–13

I once took my granddaughter with me to the mall. We passed by a store selling all types of electrical toys, and some of them were activated, roaming about near the entrance to the doorway. My granddaughter was staring at one toy in particular, a robot walking back and forth and flailing its arms. As I closely looked at the expression on her face, I realized she didn't like what she was seeing, so I asked her, "What's the matter? She said, "That robot is freaking me out." She was about four, maybe 5 years old at the time, and I didn't even know she knew what *freaking out* meant, but she did because she used the phrase correctly. Needless to say, we moved away from that store and those animated toys

There are many instances in the Bible in which I could easily understand someone freaking out over some scary or painful situation. Joseph, one of the stars in Genesis 37 and 39, comes to mind as one example. Joseph had to be extremely hurt and disheartened when his older brothers sold him into slavery because of their jealousy of him. As if that wasn't enough pain and turmoil, while enslaved he was also falsely accused of attempting to rape his master's wife and thrown into prison. Joseph didn't freak out during his time of enslavement and imprisonment, although it would have been understandable if he had done so.

Psalm 105:17–19 describes Joseph's situation this way. "He sent a man before them, even Joseph, who was sold for a servant: Whose feet they hurt with fetters: he was laid in iron: Until the time that his word came: the word of the LORD tried him." Joseph didn't know for many years why God had allowed so much trouble to enter his life. Before this seemingly impossible situation, he was the golden child and the apple of his father's eye. Later Joseph understood that his enslavement and imprisonment were the catalyst God used to save Israel and the lives of many others during a severe famine in Egypt (Gen. 50:20).

In the book of Daniel, there's a story about Shadrach, Meshach, and Abednego. They were to be thrown into a fiery furnace by King Nebuchadnezzar because they disobeyed his mandate to worship the golden image he had set up. These young men did not freak out over the prospect of being thrown into the fire. They were very brave and full of faith. When the king approached the three men, they told Him that their God was able to save them from the fiery furnace and would deliver them, but if He didn't, they still would not serve his gods or worship his golden image (Dan. 3:16–18).

Like Joseph, they didn't know what their end would be. Also, like Joseph, they did not worry about their problem. They stayed calm and trusted God instead of freaking out. And what did God do about their predicament? He delivered them out of an atrocious situation. These young men were prime examples of how to react during the tough times. They just kept on loving and trusting God.

In 2 Chronicles 22:10–12, evil Athaliah usurped the throne of Judah when her son Ahaziah was killed. She took control of the kingdom by killing all the royal seed, those who were in line to assume the kingship in her son's stead. In her zeal to destroy all the princes of Judah, she missed one, Joash, her grandson. Athaliah's daughter, Jehoshabeath saw what her mother had done and went into action, taking the baby prince from among the king's sons that had been murdered. Jehoshabeath could have freaked out over this situation but she didn't. She remained level-headed and hid her little nephew, Joash along with his nurse in a bedchamber. He remained with Jehoshabeath and her husband, Jehoiada, for six years while Athaliah ruled Judah. When the child turned seven, he was anointed king of Judah, and Athaliah was slain.

We live in a fallen world, and because of this we're all going to suffer some degree of pain and discomfort; whether we're Christians or non-Christians. If while alive you committed your life to Christ, on Judgment Day you will receive a reward for your faithfulness. If you're not born again you've suffered for nothing, but that doesn't have to be the end of your story. If you're not born again or if you're not sure of your status with Christ you can rectify that problem right now. Pray this prayer.

Heavenly Father, save me. Forgive me for all my sins and make me a new creature in Christ. Teach me Your ways and how to please You. Lord, I thank You in advance for this blessing. In Jesus's name, I pray. Amen.

## 26

# WHO LOVES YA, BABY?

For God so loved the world, that he gave his only
begotten Son, that whosoever believeth in him
should not perish, but have everlasting life.
—John 3:16

The catchphrase "Who loves ya, baby?" was used by
Telly Savalas in a TV show of the '70s called *Kojak*. It was
tucked in the back of my mind for years, and I didn't think
about it until the phrase resurfaced last week while I was
concentrating on this scripture. As I read it, the perfect
answer to the phrase "Who loves ya baby?" is—God does.
He loves us not because of who we are but because of who
He is. He is love, and He loves us.

Have you ever had a pity party and maybe just for a
moment you felt God no longer loved you? Many, many
years ago when I was driving home from work one morning
that very thought entered my mind. I had been depressed,
and I remember saying to myself, "I guess God doesn't love
me anymore." Immediately after uttering those words, my
car spun around on Nostrand and Atlantic Avenues, and

I lost control of it. My heart was beating fast while this was going on because it was rush hour and the roads were crowded with cars and people crossing the streets back and forth. I was so afraid.

As unbelievable as it may seem, this incident covered two or three of the traffic lanes, and yet God didn't let me hit any pedestrians or have an accident with another car. On top of that, I was in a backslidden state. I had stopped going to church, and I no longer prayed or read my Bible. I thought of myself more than I thought of God, and yet He still loved me.

When my car finally stopped, it was facing the opposite direction of the way I was originally traveling. I knew my car spinning around in traffic was no coincidence. I had just been corrected because of what I had said about God not loving me anymore. I never said or thought such foolishness ever again. How could I have thought so in the first place? He sent His only Son, Jesus, to die on the Cross for me.

Many of us believe love means having strong, positive feelings for someone, and it does, but it doesn't stop there. Love is more than an emotional attachment or feeling. Some people use the word *love* so flippantly, not realizing that it isn't always mushy or easy. Just ask Jesus how mushy love was when He was hanging on the Cross. Oh, it's easy to love that special someone when that person isn't constantly hurting you or disappointing you, but let that person give you nothing but grief, and see how long that deep love lasts. That's when it's hard.

There are people who keep loving their significant others even in extremely difficult situations, but some people cannot do this. This may be the reason the divorce rate is so high in the United States. We are human beings, and apart from God, our love is limited and flawed. First Corinthians 13:4–8a is recited at some weddings. I'm not sure those who recite these words realize that in this chapter Apostle Paul describes love as a spiritual gift, and without God's help we can't love this way.

I think it's kind of funny in an odd sort of way how some people compare their relationships to others who received cards, flowers, etc. on Valentine's Day. They become upset because they didn't receive any of the trimmings associated with this "love day" as their friends or coworkers did. If they could just grasp the truth about love—that it is not spelled g-i-f-t-s on February 14—they would possibly have a better day. And here's a thought: If you're not in a relationship, nothing's wrong with doing something special for yourself on that day, or any day for that matter.

Valentine's Day is wonderful, and I applaud whoever was responsible for making it a day to celebrate love, but it is not the epitome of what love truly is. Love is not a *one-day-a-year* occurrence. It is more about what you do for someone than what you say to them. Love is forgiving someone and not throwing that thing back in their face. It is nursing the sick and feeding the poor. Sometimes you have to give tough love. You have to be stern with someone when you don't want to be. It is also loving your enemy as Jesus spoke about in Matthew 5:44. Christ knew about enemies; He had some of His own. Yet He still asked God to forgive them as He hung on the Cross.

In a nutshell, love is the way Jesus Christ feels about you and me. He said in John 15:13: "Greater love hath no man than this, that a man lay down his life for his friends."

That's what Jesus did when He was crucified; He laid down His life for His friends (us). Another passage, Romans 5:7–8 says: "For scarcely for a righteous man will one die: yet peradventure for a good man some would even dare to die. But God commendeth his love toward us, in that, while we were yet sinners, Christ died for us." Both these verses show how deeply He loves us.

One of my favorite biblical passages is Romans 8:38–39 which says: "For I am persuaded, that neither death, nor life, nor angels, nor principalities, nor powers, nor things present, nor things to come, Nor height, nor depth, nor any other creature, shall be able to separate us from the love of God, which is in Christ Jesus our Lord." Nothing can separate us from His love. God has always loved us. His love through Christ has paved the way for us to live eternally with Him in a most beautiful place, where we'll have no more pain and sorrow. The Bible says He'll wipe away all tears from our eyes (Rev. 21:4). We'll have new bodies and a new home. We'll even have a new name given to us by Jesus Christ (Rev. 2:17).

John 3:16 says God loves the entire world. That includes the backslider too. No matter who you are God loves you and wants a personal relationship with you. Are you in a backslidden state? Maybe you've never accepted Christ as your Savior. He loves you, and He wants to save you. Make Him your choice today. Pray this prayer with me.

Heavenly Father, I want to be saved. I want Jesus Christ to be my Lord and Savior. I need help; I'm tired of the life I'm living. Save me, Lord. And forgive me of all my sins. Thank You, God, for hearing my prayer, and for loving me the way You do. In the name of Jesus, I pray. Amen.

# 27

# LORD, I'LL TAKE THE CRUMBS

And there was a certain beggar named Lazarus,
which was laid at his gate, full of sores, And
desiring to be fed with the crumbs which fell from
the rich man's table: moreover the dogs came and
licked his sores.

—Luke 16:20, 21:20

Lazarus the beggar was in a poor state. He was hungry, and he laid at the rich man's gate hoping for some crumbs which fell from his table. He had a lot of sores on his body but at present his main concern was for food. I can picture him begging the rich man as he finished his meal, "Can I have the crumbs, please sir?" Lazarus had no aversion to them, and neither did a woman in Mark, chapter 7.

This woman used the analogy about crumbs when seeking healing for her daughter. Mark 7:26–29 states: "The woman was a Greek, a Syrophoenician by nation; and she besought him that he would cast forth the devil out of her daughter. But Jesus said unto her, Let the children first be filled: for it is not meet to take the children's bread, and to cast it unto the dogs. And she answered and said unto him, Yes, Lord: yet the dogs under the table eat of the children's crumbs. And he said unto her, For this saying go thy way; the devil is gone out of thy daughter."

If we are to be perfectly honest, many of us think of crumbs as insignificant specks of food to be discarded as waste. If crumbs have fallen onto the kitchen table from our plates, we dispose of them into the garbage can. If someone dared to offer us crumbs, we might be offended. There are people, not everyone, but some people who enjoy crumbs more than the intact product.

I've seen one or maybe two people crumble their crackers into their soup on purpose. The value of the crumb is not lost on them. Neither is it lost on the animal kingdom. I've watched pigeons pecking away at crumbs on the sidewalks, and for them, the crumbs appear to be a smorgasbord. If they could talk, I can imagine them saying, "I'll take the crumbs," or maybe "Thank You, Lord, for the crumbs." Their actions certainly profess this sentiment.

Lazarus understood the importance of crumbs as sustenance for his body. The mother valued them as healing for her daughter, and the pigeons saw the crumbs simply as food. Jesus, more than anyone, knew the importance of crumbs. When He fed the five thousand people, He had His disciples gather the fragments left over, which amounted to twelve baskets of food. His reasoning was "so that nothing would be lost" (John 6:12). I wonder how many people were fed from those baskets full of leftovers. I also wonder how many of us would have snubbed our noses at those fragments if we didn't know they were part of a miracle from the Lord.

One of my earliest memories about crumbs came from the German fairytale *Hansel and Gretel*. The brother and sister of the story had been abandoned in the dark woods by their father. The stepmom had forced their father to leave them there because of her fear of not having enough to eat because of a famine. The kids overheard this conversation so Hansel sneaked outside to gather pebbles. He dropped the pebbles on the way to the forest so that they could find their way back home. When the kids returned home the next day the stepmom was angry. She forced the father to take them back to the forest. This time Hansel dropped breadcrumbs. He and his sister returned home again but not because of the crumbs. The birds had eaten them up. Those birds knew the value of crumbs and so did the author of the story.

God is constantly blessing us, and if He has given what you consider to be crumbs, be thankful for them because little is much in the Master's hands. Just look at the widow God sent Elijah to. Who do you think blessed her to have that small pot of oil to begin with? And when the appointed time came, God increased it so much that she was able to sell some of it and pay off the debt and live on the rest (2 Kings 4). What a pension plan that was!

There are possibly millions of people all over the world, and many of them right here in America, who would give their *eyeteeth* to have just a little of the "crumbs" we take for granted. For those who don't know what eyeteeth are, according to the Colgate website, these teeth are "the longest, strongest, most stable, and most prominent teeth in your mouth." I've heard some call them vampire teeth.

Jesus knew the value of crumbs. He didn't disdain the leftovers or crumbs after feeding the four thousand and the five thousand groups of people. He had His disciples gather up what was left. He didn't personally need the food fragments. After all, He's God the Son. He owns everything. If crumbs are valuable to the Lord, how important do you think we humans are to Him? We were all created out of love, and because He loves us so much, He did something amazing for us. He gave His life so that we could be reconciled to the Father and live eternally with Him in a place He's specifically preparing for us.

First Timothy 2:4b says: "God's desire is that all men be saved, and come to the knowledge of the truth." He's not offering crumbs here; He's offering you life eternal. He won't force you to take it or make you pay for it. You couldn't afford it anyway. There's no way, we could pay the price for our sins or the sins of the world, but Jesus did just that when He shed His blood on the Cross.

Won't you accept His gift of love? His salvation is freely given and is the best gift you have ever been offered. Accept His gift today by asking Him to forgive you for your sins and to be your Savior. What do you gain in return? More than you could ever imagine, which includes, but is not limited to, eternal life. In God's time you will live in His presence. There'll be no more having to wrestle with sin because Satan will have been cast into the lake of fire. There'll be happiness and joy galore, no more sickness and no pain. Do you have a better offer? Jesus is waiting. What's it going to be?

Acknowledge Him and ask Him to save you, to be your Lord and Savior. However you choose to word the apology for sinning and rejecting Him, ask for His forgiveness, and He will give it to you. There's no waiting period after you say those words. You'll immediately become a born-again Christian, destined for a great future.

## 28

# O TASTE AND SEE

O taste and see that the LORD is good: blessed is
the man that trusteth in him.

—Psalm 34:8

This psalm was written by King David who knew firsthand how good the Lord is, and he didn't want to keep this good news all to himself. He was in a relationship with the Lord from an early age, and this connection continued for as long as he lived. In Psalm 37:25 David said, "I have been young, and now am old; yet have I not seen the righteous forsaken, nor his seed begging bread." If David were alive today, I believe he would still be singing that same song of never having been disappointed by God. This psalm encourages me to trust the Lord as David did.

David not only relied on the Lord for food, shelter, protection, and deliverance, but God was his All and all. Everything he needed was summed up in God as his Source. Before becoming king of Israel, David's occupation was a shepherd. While he was looking after his family's sheep, God was looking after him. Because David learned early to rely on the Lord, he had no fear when facing a bear and a lion, which came to snatch a lamb from his flock. I don't know anyone personally who would confront a hungry wild animal, but David did. He went after that lion and bear like the warrior God was grooming him to be. He slew them and rescued the lamb (1 Sam. 17:34–36).

These victories were some of the events that gave David practice and courage to trust the Lord in any situation. In a famous story in the Bible, David stood up to Goliath, a giant who was threatening the Israelites, talking about what he was going to do to them and to David. David was not deterred by Goliath's words. He had some of his own.

In 1 Samuel 34:45–47, David let this smack-talking Philistine know that the God he served was going to deliver the giant into his hands, and God did just that. I admire David's faith. Before the battle with Goliath had even started, David had faith that God would come to his rescue. He knew that this battle belonged to the Lord and that it was already won. What was his faith based on? It was based on his many experiences of God never failing him. David constantly tasted and saw that the Lord is good and I believe this is one of the reasons he wrote this psalm, to spread the word of God's goodness to others.

To accept King David's invitation to taste and see the goodness of the Lord is to experience unimaginable pleasures and joys, not just when you go to heaven, but while you're here on earth too (Prov. 11:31a). Tasting and seeing is communing with God intimately. It is knowing that He hears your every word and will answer you back. It's a chance to see how He will supply all your needs as Apostle Paul says He will in Philippians 4:19. Tasting and seeing is the opportunity to have dreams come true that you never thought were possible (Eph. 3:20). and it is an invite to see how "No weapon that is formed against thee shall prosper" when an enemy attacks you (Isa. 54:17). God is exceptional and excellent.

O taste and see! O taste and see! He's so loving toward us that many times He'll answer us before we call Him, and while we're yet speaking, He'll hear us (Isa. 65:24). God is so magnanimous toward us that He takes care of the saved as well as the unsaved. Matthew 5:45 says so. He's so wonderful that He sacrificed His only Son to die in our place so that we might be reconciled to Him. He forgives us of our despicable sins, and He never reminds us of who we used to be. O taste and see that the Lord is good!

The day came when I took King David's advice and tasted for myself how good God is. I should have come to Him sooner. He had been calling me, but I didn't want to be saved yet, so I kept stalling. I knew or at least I thought I knew that I'd get saved one day when I was old. How silly of me. Here I was thinking it was all up to me. Meanwhile, I was rejecting what I didn't even understand, and I told God that I thought being saved would be boring. This was no secret to God. He's omniscient. He knows everything. He didn't get mad at me or punish me for my thoughts; instead, He continued to call me to Him. He knew I was being tricked by Satan, who if he had his way, I would have died not knowing Jesus Christ as my Savior.

On April 2, 1999, I attended a Good Friday service to hear my daughter and future godson speak at a Seven Last Words service. I had no intention of getting saved that day, but something miraculous happened to me. As the Reverend

Felicia Faye Long made the altar call, I could literally taste something in my mouth, and it tasted so good. Did I say so good? I meant soooo good. I had never tasted anything like it before. The only way I can explain it is that when I was in high school, we learned about Greek and Roman mythology. I don't know why, but one of the things that stuck with me was that these so-called gods ate nectar and ambrosia. In my mind, that meant there wasn't anything more exquisite to dine on. I had nothing else to compare the sensation going on in my mouth with, so for me the nectar and ambrosia fit that description perfectly.

As I tasted what seemed like the words Rev. Long was speaking, I said to God, "This tastes so good." God spoke to me and said, "Why don't you come down to the altar and give your life to me?" I looked around and said, "Lord, ain't nobody else getting up." He answered, "Why don't you break the ice and be the first one." I could no longer reject His offer of salvation, so I went down there in obedience to Him. I wasn't sorry for my sins yet, because as I said I wasn't ready to be saved, but when I knelt at that altar, the Holy Spirit began to do a work in my heart, and the waterworks began. I cried and cried while asking for forgiveness of my sins. I felt like my heart was breaking as I knelt before the Lord. I was a little anxious too, because in the back of my mind I didn't think they had enough tissue for all my tears and runny nose, but thank God they did.

After I finished crying and accepting the Lord's salvation, I stood and looked around. To my surprise, the altar was full of others who came to the altar after I did. I believe they too wanted to taste and see how good the Lord is. How wrong I was about salvation. It's not boring at all.

It's a wonderful life of being loved by God, being taught, guided, and used by Him, and yes, it is exciting. I thank my God that He chose me before the foundation of the world (Eph. 1:4)

Psalm 100:5 says: "For the Lord is good; his mercy is everlasting; and his truth endureth to all generations." Like the psalmist, I am a witness that the Lord is good. Have you ever noticed how some people get excited in the presence of the president or a favorite actor or musical artist? They don't know them personally, and yet they want to take a picture with them. God is greater than any president, actor, or artist, and yet many people push Him away. The amazing thing about God is that He loves us anyway. That's how good He is. He loves us and He wants a relationship with us.

If you don't have a relationship with the Lord, have you given thought to it? I know some are putting it off just as I did, but believe me, you don't know what you're missing. God is a loving Father who only wants the best for you. Whether you know it or not, there is a void deep inside of you that only He can fill. Won't you give Him a chance to fill it? Won't you taste and see how good He is? If your answer is yes, just ask the Lord to come into your heart and forgive you for your sins. Tell Him you're sorry for all you've done. Thank Him because He forgave you immediately. Now you are born again. Hallelujah, praise God!

# 29

# WHY ME?

Blessed be the God and Father of our Lord Jesus
Christ, who has blessed us with every spiritual
blessing in the heavenly places in Christ, just as
He chose us in Him before the foundation of
the world, that we should be holy and without
blame before Him in love, having predestined us
to adoption as sons by Jesus Christ to Himself,
according to the good pleasure of His will, to
the praise of the glory of His grace, by which He
made us accepted in the Beloved.
—Ephesians 1:3–6

To understand these verses is to realize just how blessed
we are, how special we are to God. He has blessed us in so
many ways with spiritual and earthly blessings. Before the
world was even formed, He had already chosen us to be His
adopted children. He has done and is doing so much for us
in the spiritual realm that we can't grasp or understand it all.
God is constantly blessing us with earthly blessings too, and
if we were to try to count each one of them, our list of what

He's done for us would be sorely lacking. So this brings me to the question, "Why, Lord, do you love me so much? Why did You die on the Cross for me? Why do you heap countless blessings upon me?" I am, imperfect, you know that I am, and yet you treat me as if I'm not, and I must say that most of the time I feel like I'm your favorite child. Why me?

I can imagine David having a similar thought about God when He made him the king of Israel. This was an extreme change for the shepherd boy. He must have been overwhelmed that God would choose him for such a task. He could hardly handle the idea of being King Saul's son-in -law. At first, he refused the offer but when Saul gave him a task to gain his daughter it seemed more palpable to him. When Samuel anointed David king of Israel, did he ask himself, "Why me?" I could certainly understand if he did.

First Peter 2:9 tells me we are really special. It says that "But ye are a chosen generation, a royal priesthood, an holy nation, a peculiar people." This scripture says the reason we have been chosen is to declare God's praise. That's really something; to be singled out by the Creator of the universe. Sometimes it's hard for me to grasp that God would choose me.

He is so loving and wonderful that when I think of the billions upon billions of people who were born from the very beginning of time up to today, I can't help but ask the question, "Why me? Why did you choose me to be one of your children; one who will one day live better than any rich person living on the earth ever could? Why is my future so wonderfully unfathomable when my time on this earth is done? I haven't done anything to earn your love. It can't be earned. I was born with a sinful nature, and yet you see me as special. David touched on this sinful nature in Psalm

51:5. He said, "I was shapen in iniquity and in sin did my mother conceive me." And yet God still chose him, chose us.

David didn't take God's love for granted, and neither will I. When I ask the question, "Why me?" I'm not expecting a response. This is a rhetorical question. I already know the answer. When I ask "Why me?" it is my way of marveling at the magnitude of God's love for me. It is my way of voicing my amazement of all He does for, to, and through me. First John 3:1 says: "Behold, what manner of love the Father hath bestowed upon us, that we should be called the sons of God." We could never love Him as much as He loves us, but we can surely try.

If you've been trying to do good instead of getting saved it won't work. You could never be that good, and your goodness could never compare to the blood Christ shed on the Cross. In John 5:30 Jesus said: "I can of mine own self do nothing: as I hear, I judge: and my judgment is just; because I seek not mine own will, but the will of the Father which hath sent me." Why did He sacrifice His life for us? It's simple: *love*. Are you willing to love Him back? Loving Him means obeying Him (John 14:15). You can't do this on your own but He will help you. That's one of the reasons He sent His Holy Spirit. Come to Him now. He's waiting for you with open arms. If you're ready, pray with me.

Heavenly Father, You did such a great thing for me by sending Your Son, Jesus Christ, to die on the Cross for me. I am so sorry for my sins, and I apologize for all of them. Forgive me, Lord, and save me. I want to be born again. I accept Your gift, dear Lord, and I am so grateful to you. In the blessed name of Jesus Christ, I pray. Amen.

# 30

# THE RAPTURE

For the Lord himself shall descend from heaven
with a shout, with the voice of the archangel, and
with the trump of God: and the dead in Christ
shall rise first: Then we which are alive and
remain shall be caught up together with them in
the clouds, to meet the Lord in the air: and so
shall we ever be with the Lord. (Amen).
—1 Thessalonians 4:16–17

Have you ever wondered how it would feel to sail through the air freely? You rise into the clouds with no benefit of an airplane, a helicopter, or a hot-air balloon. There's nothing attached to you, and you're not attached to anything that would pull you upward into the stratosphere. Seems impossible, right? But the time will come when that very thing will happen, at least to some of us. One day Jesus Christ will come for the saints of God, and we're going to be caught up to meet Him in the air.

Another scripture, in Hebrews 9:28 (NIV), says: " So Christ was sacrificed once to take away the sins of many; and he will appear a second time, not to bear sin, but to bring salvation to those who are waiting for him." All you born-again believers rest assured that you will not be left behind when Jesus comes to rapture or whisk His church away to be with Him. Some people believe the Rapture will take place before the Tribulation period mentioned in the book of Revelation, and others believe it will take place during or after this period. There are also those who don't believe it will happen at all. Whatever your belief about the Rapture, this wonderful occurrence has been planned for a very long time, and the invitation and ability to participate in it comes from the Lord Jesus Christ, Himself.

The Rapture or *harpazo* (Greek translation) is going to be so wonderful that I suspect it would blow our minds if the Lord didn't give us glorified bodies to absorb the excitement and joy of it all. According to the *Strongest NIV Exhaustive Concordance*, harpazo means to catch, steal, carry off. It also means snatched up or to take by force. Any of those definitions are all right with me because they all convey that Jesus Christ is keeping His promise to come back for me—to take me to be with Him.

I get excited when I think about 1 Thessalonians 4:13–18. I try to imagine what it will be like if I'm alive when these scriptures of Jesus coming in the clouds are fulfilled. One second, I'll be on the earth, the only home I've ever known, and the next thing I'll experience is *swoosh*, being in the sky with Jesus Christ and a great multitude of Christians from all nationalities and walks of life. For those who have been Raptured, death and sickness will be a thing of the past.

Revelation 21:4 says: "And God shall wipe away all tears

from their eyes; and there shall be no more death, neither sorrow, nor crying, neither shall there be any more pain: for the former things are passed away." No negative thing will be a part of the fabric of our future home, which Jesus has prepared for those who love Him. There is a saying that "if something sounds too good to be true it probably is." That's not the case for the Rapture. It sounds too good to be true, but it is true, and it is going to take place just as Jesus Christ promised.

No earthly experience you can think about or dream of can compare to the heavenly bliss awaiting those who have accepted Christ as their Lord and Savior. The Rapture is going to be an "out of this world experience." Born-again believers will be transported to a new home, to a place more awesome than anything any of us has seen on earth. This is going to be an amazing time, a time that never ends.

.For the thrill-seekers, who are always looking for the next adrenaline rush, you haven't experienced anything like the Rapture. For drug addicts, who are always chasing that feeling they got from their first high, this event will make chasing that high seem like the dumbest thing they've ever chased. No matter how rich you may be, you don't have enough money to buy the feelings of happiness and well-being that you'll experience once Christ comes for you.

Are you lonely? Do you yearn for friends or family? Giving your life to Christ and being Raptured will guarantee you'll have a permanent family, and you will never feel lonely again. You'll now become a part of the biggest family reunion of all time. Many of these individuals were members of your earthly family. Some were your friends, neighbors and coworkers. You will meet some individuals who died centuries ago, and others may have died more recently. So many people, and you have eternity to get to know them all.

The timing of their deaths is unimportant. The important thing is that if they accepted Christ as their Savior before they passed away; they too will be raptured, and just for the record, if you happen to be alive at Christ's return, those saints who passed away previously will be in the clouds before you will. This isn't something to be concerned about though because the Bible says the Rapture will take place in a moment, in the twinkling of an eye. It further teaches that we will not all sleep, but we will all be changed (1 Cor. 15:51–52).

The bottom line is that if you're born again, you'll be included in this magnificent gathering in the clouds. Something else worth mentioning is that when Jesus comes for us, He'll give us glorified bodies that will last for eternity. With these glorified bodies, we'll be able to see God face-to-face, which we can't do presently (Rev. 22:4). I once heard someone say that at Christ's coming, we'll get an upgrade of our bodies. You may have lost a limb, an eye, your teeth, you may be ill or suffering from all sorts of aches and pains; whatever the case may be, when Christ comes back for you, He will give you a new body, and to use an old phrase, it will be "brand spanking new." According to 1 Corinthians 15:35–38, it won't be the old body you had while on earth. This scripture says we'll be given bodies like the resurrected Christ, and let me tell you, you can't get any better than that.

In the meantime, until Christ comes back for us, we have work to do. Born-again believers, we need to tell others about the Lord—that He's God's Son, and that He died on the Cross for us so that we might be reconciled to God the Father. Jesus was a walking, talking, living testimony to the power of God while on the earth, and we can be that way too. Jesus is coming back. Don't you want to be one of those He's coming back for? Don't you want to experience the love He's offering? And don't you want a body, and a life, free from pain and disappointment? If your answer is yes to either of these questions, pray this prayer with me.

Dear Lord, I thank You for Your kindness and all the blessings You constantly bestow upon me daily. I confess that Jesus is Lord. I believe He died on the Cross and You raised Him from the dead. Save me, Lord, forgive me of all my sins. Heal, deliver, and set me free from this present life of not knowing you personally. Thank You, Lord. In the blessed name of Jesus, I pray. Amen.

## 31

# THE SECOND COMING OF CHRIST

For yourselves know perfectly that the day of the
Lord so cometh as a thief in the night. For when
they shall say, Peace and safety; then sudden
destruction cometh upon them, as travail upon a
woman with child; and they shall not escape.
—1 Thessalonians 5:2–3

"Jesus is coming like a thief in the night and no man knows the day or the hour." You don't hear this warning too much in the pulpit nowadays, but when I was a kid, I heard it a lot. In a 1984 movie titled *The Terminator*, Arnold Schwarzenegger coined the phrase, "I'll be back." As popular as this phrase is, Schwarzenegger was not the first person to make such a statement. Jesus Christ said He would be back, centuries before Arnold or the writer of the movie was even born. Jesus's promise to come back is a most serious truth spoken by One who never lies.

Let's read another scripture concerning the Second Coming. It reads," Behold, he cometh with clouds; and every eye shall see him, and they also which pierced him:

and all kindreds of the earth shall wail because of him. Even so, Amen" (Rev. 1:7). Quite a few scriptures warn of this event. No one knows when it will take place except God the Father, not even the angels in heaven (Matt. 24:36). The Second Coming will take place after the Rapture and the Tribulation period, which will last for seven years. Christ warns us of His return in the Word so that we will be prepared. It is also a warning to the unsaved. Now is the time to give your life to the Lord (before it's too late).

Let me slow down just a little and explain the three events of the future. The Rapture is when Christ catches the born-again believers up into the clouds to be with Him forever (1 Thess. 4:16–17). The Tribulation period is the next step in this chain of events (Rev. chapters 5–9). This period will be filled with pain and torture of the inhabitants left on the earth who did not accept Christ as their Savior before the Rapture. The third event, the Second Coming, which is the topic of this sermon; is when Christ comes back to the earth to set up His Messianic kingdom (Rev. 19:1–21). Other descriptions of the Second Coming are found in John 14:2–3 and Acts 1:9–11, as well as in a few other books of the Bible. You must read about these events carefully because some end-time passages can be confusing, seemingly pointing to any one of the three occurrences previously mentioned here.

Many people don't know about God's plans for the end time because they haven't spent time reading His Word. Some aren't concerned about it because they don't believe God exists, and they don't believe Jesus is coming back. Second Peter 3:3–4 says: "Knowing this first, that there shall come in the last days scoffers, walking after their own lusts, And saying, Where is the promise of his coming? for since the fathers fell asleep, all things continue as they were from the beginning of the creation." Someone else may ask, "If He's coming back, what's taking Him so long?" Peter must have anticipated these questions. In 2 Peter 3:9 he says: "The Lord is not slack concerning his promise, as some men count slackness; but is longsuffering to us-ward, not willing that any should perish, but that all should come to repentance."

God's Word says Jesus is coming back, and I believe it. Will He be coming back for you? Will you die not having received Him as your Savior? If you're reading this sermon, Christ has not yet returned, and you still can ensure your future in heaven with Him. He said in Revelation 3:20: "Behold, I stand at the door, and knock: if any man hear my voice, and open the door, I will come in to him, and will sup with him, and he with me." Jesus is calling you to Himself. He wants to be your Savior. He wants to forever show His love for you like no other person on earth ever has or ever could.

John 3:16 says God sent Jesus, His only begotten Son, to die on the Cross for our sins. Don't refuse this gift of everlasting love. Whether we will live in heaven with Him or in hell eternally depends on the decision we make to accept or reject His offer of salvation while we live. If you don't believe this, you're not alone; lots of people. Albert Einstein, who was considered a genius, once said, "Just because you don't believe in something doesn't mean it isn't true." Not believing in Christ doesn't make Him nonexistent, and it doesn't make what He promised untrue.

There's something called erring on the side of caution.

This means making a "safe" choice instead of a risky one or choosing the path that won't harm you or cause a problem if you're wrong. Not accepting Christ as your Savior is a huge mistake, the biggest one you could ever make. Eternity is a long time to regret not making the choice to accept Christ as your Savior. If you would like to be saved and have a personal relationship with Christ, pray this prayer with me.

Dear Lord, I need You. I need You as my Lord and Savior. I repent of all my sins, and I ask You to forgive me and save me. I believe that You heard me, and I thank You. In the blessed name of Jesus Christ, amen.

PS: For the record, some scholars do not believe in the time frame of the Rapture, the Tribulation period, and afterward the Second Coming of Christ. Some believe the Rapture and Second Coming are the same. No problem. Our salvation is not based on our agreement on when these events will occur. It's based on the fact that Christ died on the Cross to atone for our sins, and we have accepted Him as our Savior.

## 32

# THANK YOU, LORD

O give thanks unto the Lord; for he is good; for
his mercy endureth for ever.

—1 Chronicles 16:34

Thank You, Lord, for everything. Thank You for being You. Thank You for loving me and for sending Your Son to die on the Cross for me. Thank You, Jesus for sacrificing Your life for not only me but for all of mankind. Thank You, Holy Spirit, for comforting, guiding, and teaching me how I should live. Thank You Lord for saving me and never giving up on me. Thank You for ordering my steps and helping me to obey your Word. Thank You that although I'm not perfect, you encourage me every day to do my best to be who You called me to be.

Thank You, God, for forgiving me for every sin I've ever committed. Thank You for forgiving me for the present and future ones too. Thank You, Lord for never throwing them back in my face. Thank You for my new shelf life; unlike expired food, I won't ever be discarded. I get another chance to not just survive but to thrive all throughout eternity. Thank You for showing Your great love for me every single day.

Thank You for intervening to save my life when I couldn't do anything to save myself. You once kept me from drowning, and numerous times You saved me from car accidents that I believe would have resulted in me losing my life. I know that there are and were many times I wasn't aware of Your protection, and I'm so grateful that You have always looked out for me. You're so amazing. Thank You, thank You, thank You. Thank You, Lord, for the plans You have for me on earth, and thank You for the plans You have for me when I get to heaven. Thank You for giving me a hunger for Your Word. Thank You for giving me opportunities to tell others about You. Thank You for Your everyday mercies, and thank You that they never fail.

Thank You for all my family members. Thank You for putting me in this family, a big loving family. Thank You for my church family too. Thank You for my friends, those I've known for years, and those who are relatively new. Thank You for those who were in my life for a reason, some for a season, and others for a lifetime. Thank You for my enemies too. They make me stronger, and thank You for opening my eyes to see how You've often protected me from them. Thank You for kind neighbors.

Thank You, Lord, for my pastors who are visionaries. I learned a lot sitting under their leadership. Your kingdom is enriched because of their faithfulness, and so am I. Thank You for the wisdom and knowledge You pour into me daily, and thank You for the teachers, preachers, and professors you assigned to my growth in You so that I could minister to others. Thank You for scientists; health-care workers, teachers, janitors, cooks—and all the people who make life easier for the entire world. Thank You for giving the medical field knowledge and wisdom to operate and perform all types of procedures to heal and prolong life.

Thank You, Lord, for my life, health, and strength. Thank you for the activity of my limbs. Thank You for giving me clarity of mind. Thank You for all the times You've healed me. Thank You for always providing for me. Thank You for food. Thank You for shelter. Thank You for my memory, the things I do remember, and thank You for the things I don't remember. Some of my healing has come because of what I don't remember, but most of my healing has taken place because of what I do remember. Thank You for waking me up each day.

Thank You for my tears. My tears have relieved my body of pent-up stress, which otherwise might have contributed to ailments caused by holding in too much pain and worry. I also thank You for my tears because my crying has been a part of my learning many painful lessons. Thank You for laughter too. It makes us feel good, and it is a great stress breaker. What a wonderful gift! I am enriched because of my tears and my laughter. Lord, I thank You for sight, for sound, for being able to speak, and for being able to touch people.

Thank You for the animals, foliage, and flowers. Thank You for the gift of smell and taste. Thank You for the wind and the rain. Thank You for music and poetry. Thank You for the alphabet, and thank You for cellphones, which enable us to communicate with people near and far. Thank You for televisions, computers, washing machines, cars, buses, trains, and airplanes.

Thank You for Your favor upon my life. Thank You for the jobs I've had. Thank You for prompting me to go to college and seminary. Thank You for allowing me to do well in my schooling. Thank you for Rev. E. Suber. I will be forever grateful to her for making it possible for me to be accepted into seminary. Thank You for Vivian Hernandez, who agreed to mentor me while doing my internship. Thank You for her excellence as she took me under her wing. Thank You also for Pastor Mike Corbin who allowed me to complete the remaining hours I needed for my internship at the men's shelter. I'm so grateful for all the people you put in my pathway to help me.

Thank You for taking some of my family members home to be with You. You took away their pain and suffering. Thank You for the peace I feel knowing that I will one day see them again.

Thank You, Lord, for my trials and my troubles. All that You have allowed has taught me that Your Word is true. Thank you that now I understand that all things do work together for good even if I don't understand how. Thank You for teaching me to trust You. Thank You for the times I feel great and for when I've had to pray through my problems and at times ailments. How would I have known You to be my Healer and my Helper if things were always going well?

Thank You for all of Your communication with me. Thank You for being omnipresent, omnipotent, and omniscient. Thank You for knowing everything about me and loving me anyway. Thank You for my gifts and talents, even those not yet discovered. This is just a minuscule portion of all that I thank You for. I could go on and on, and even then I'd miss much and most of what You've done for me. You've been just that good. For all that isn't mentioned, I thank You, Lord, for everything.

Do you have something to thank God for? Of course, you do, and it doesn't matter whether you're saved or not because the Bible says, "it rains on the just as well as the unjust" (Matt. 5:45). That means God also looks out for and blesses those who aren't saved. Are you born again? If not, you can be. If you've been touched by this discourse and have decided to make Jesus your Savior, ask the Lord to save you. He'll do it immediately. If you've asked for His forgiveness, if you've asked Him to be your Savior, you can thank Him right now because He did what you asked Him to do. I would like to thank Him with you. Thank You, Lord, for saving another soul and adding another family member to Your kingdom. We praise You and love You. Amen.

# Works Cited

*Bruce Almighty*. Directed by Tom Shadyac. (Universal Pictures, 2003).

Clarke, Adam. "Commentary on Psalms 145:3." *The Adam Clarke Commentary*. https://www.studylight.org/commentaries/acc/psalms-145.html. 1832.

Goodrick, Edward W, et al. *The Strongest NIV Exhaustive Concordance*. Grand Rapids, MI: Zondervan, 1999, p. 1532. Print.

Hansel and Gretel, Brothers Grimm 1812.

https://biblehub.com>commentaries.

https://www.colgate.com/en-us/oral-health/mouth ... 16 August 2022.

https://www.dictionary.com.

https://www.goodreads.com/quotes/144557-resentment-is-like-drinking-poison-and-then-hoping-it-will. 19 April 2022.

https://www.goodreads.com/author/quotes/459689. Marlene Dietrich. 19 April 2022.

https://www.goodreads.com/quotes/714001-the-robin-and-the-sparrow-said-the-robin-to-the

https://www.goodreads.com/quotes/726216-rule-no-1-is-don-t-sweat-the-small-stuff-rule. 21 June 2022.

http://www.goodreads.com/quotes/881782-just-because-you-don-t-believe-in-somethi ... 22 June 2022.

https://history.house.gov/Historical-Highlights/1951-2000/The-legislation-placing-%E2%80%9CIn-God-We-Trust%E2%80%9D-on-national-currency/.

https://inspire99.com/every-problem-is-a-gift-anthony-robbins.

https://www.quoteslyfe.com/quote/When-I-look-back-on-all-these-239428. 21 June 2022.

https://www.studylight.org/commentaries/eng/pnt/john-10.html?msclkid=1432e1d8a92711ecad84935260ad0d9a. 1891.). Assessed 22 March 2022.

Jeffrey Woods, director. "Broken Vows, Bloody Murder." *Fatal Attraction*, season 1, episode 2, IMDb, 2013.

*Kojak.* Created by Abby Mann. (1973–78; Universal Television).

Lenzner, Robert. "Bernie Madoff's $50 Billion Ponzi Scheme." Forbes Magazine, 12 Dec. 2008. Accessed 13 April 2022.

Mississippi Mass Choir. "I Just Can't Tell It All." *Mississippi Mass Choir: Greatest Hits.* Malaco Inc., 1995.

pubmed.ncbi.nlm.nih.gov/23878824/

*The Silence of the Lambs.* Directed by Jonathan Demme. (1991; Orion Pictures).

*The Sixth Sense.* Directed by Night M. Shyamalan. (Buena Vista Pictures Distribution, 1999).

*The Terminator.* Directed by James Cameron. (1984; Orion Pictures).

Wilmington, H. L. *Wilmington's Guide to the Bible.* Wheaton:IL. Tynsdale House, 1981, p.159. Print.